HELP YOUR CHILDREN

CHILDREN

HELP YOUR CHILDREN

John Q. Baucom, Ph.D.

PYRANEE
BOOKS

Zondervan Publishing House
Grand Rapids, Michigan

HELP YOUR CHILDREN SAY NO TO DRUGS
Copyright © 1987 by John Q. Baucom

Pyranee Books are published by Zondervan Publishing House,
1415 Lake Drive, S.E., Grand Rapids, Michigan 49506

Library of Congress Cataloging in Publication Data

Baucom, John Q.
  Help your children say no to drugs.

  "Pyranee books."
  Bibliography: p.
  1. Youth—United States—Drug use. 2. Children—United States—Drug use. 3.
Drug abuse—United States. 4. Drug abuse—United States—Prevention. I. Title.
HV5824.Y68B375   1987   649'.4   87-13356
ISBN 0-310-20901-3

Edited and designed by Julie Ackerman Link

Printed in the United States of America

87 88 89 90 91 / DP / 10 9 8 7 6 5 4 3 2 1

CONTENTS

ACKNOWLEDGMENTS

Many people helped me with this book, and it is impossible to thank them all. I would, however, like to mention several by name.

Bennie, my wife, helped with the entire manuscript and had total responsibility for the questions at the end of each chapter. Without her, writing this book would have been impossible. Lois, my mother, helped tremendously by providing support and hours of discussion. Maxie Zieglar's typing and editorial input was invaluable. Others who deserve thanks include John Cupp, Jim Nobles, Doug Carl, Winferd Hendrix, Ed Lamb, and John Talbird.

I would like to add a special thanks to the more than 1,400 people I interviewed while preparing this book. I changed their names and circumstances to protect their identity, but their emotional strength and concern for others comes through strongly.

FOREWORD

"Let me help you with that," he offered.

I didn't know who he was, but I was glad for his help. The stereo turntable, receiver, and speakers that I was trying to wrestle free from the back seat of my Firebird were too much for me to carry inside in one trip. Besides, he looked strong enough and big enough to balance it all on the palm of one hand.

"Do you like basketball?" he asked as I unlocked my apartment door.

"I like watching it. I'm too uncoordinated to play."

"Do you ever go to any State games?" he asked with a sly smile.

"No," I answered truthfully, "but I go to football and hockey games." I didn't want him to think I had no school loyalty.

"Would you go if I got you some tickets?"

"Sure," I said, with a glimmer of comprehension and a hint of a smile. "I'll bet you play, don't you?"

His giggle caught me off guard. I'd never met anyone so big with such a cute little laugh. Then he smiled. A warm, proud, mischievous smile.

"Okay, so who are you?"

"You'll find out," he teased. "Your name's Julie, right? There'll be two tickets waiting for you at the box office for Saturday's game." Then he disappeared down the hallway.

That brief and mysterious encounter began my appreciation

for basketball and my fascination with a player named Terry Furlow.

I followed Michigan State basketball and Terry's career carefully after that. I attended every game. I celebrated their victories; I lamented their defeats. That year, 1976, Terry became the school's all-time leading scorer. He also scored the highest point total in one game (50) and the highest point total in one season. He was the third leading scorer in the nation, and he led the Big Ten in scoring for the second year in a row. He became a media celebrity—the bright spot in MSU sports— and a hero to local high school basketball players, especially Earvin Johnson (now known as "Magic" of the Los Angeles Lakers). Johnson once said of Terry, "Terry was like a father to me. He guided me and taught me respect for my parents and peers."

Terry and I talked frequently that season—about a lot more than just basketball. We talked about school, religion, racial problems, our families, and the pressure of living up to people's expectations. And we talked about his use of alcohol and marijuana. He claimed he used them only "to relax," to keep the pressure under control. And for all I know, he did. I never saw him drunk or high.

Back then no one was talking about drugs and athletes. If coaches or school administrators knew, they weren't telling. And if the news media knew, they too were keeping it quiet. So no one confronted Terry, and no one helped him.

Terry's reward for his incredible season came on the day of the NBA draft. I was in the kitchen with my roommates when I heard his familiar knock. I opened the door and there he stood, all six-feet, five-inches, 190 pounds of him, wearing a leather visor with "'76ers" embossed across the front. Terry appeared as cool as usual, but he couldn't hide his excitement. He'd been drafted in the first round by Philadelphia, one of the best teams in the country. We celebrated with him again.

That was our last celebration. We didn't see much of Terry after that. He still called at odd hours of the night from wherever he happened to be in the country, and he usually stopped by when he was in town, but his calls and visits became less frequent. And the celebrations ended altogether. Terry stayed with Philadelphia for just over a year, but he never got to play much. In 1977 he was traded to the Cleveland Cavaliers, then to the Atlanta Hawks, and later to the Utah Jazz. Terry was never able to live up to people's expectations in his professional career.

Four years later, after I had moved to Grand Rapids, my former roommate called early one morning with the shocking news. Terry had smashed his Mercedes into a tree somewhere near Cleveland. A newspaper article about his death said that three open beer cans and a small substance of white powder were found in the car. A brief article one month later reported that Terry "apparently had taken cocaine and Valium before his death," but the coroner said "he could not determine whether the drugs had anything to do with the crash." Back then no one was talking much about drugs and athletes.

Terry's death left me with a jumble of unanswered questions and unresolved feelings. What else should I have done for him? What more should I have said? Why didn't I try harder to keep in touch with him after he left Lansing? Would anything I could have said or done made a difference? I have never completely untangled all those thoughts and feelings. Every time I hear of another athlete with a drug problem I think again of Terry and how tragic it is that the people who loved him can no longer enjoy life with him.

Because of Terry, I jumped at the chance to publish this book when John Baucom proposed the idea for it. I saw it not only as an opportunity for John to multiply his effectiveness as a counselor and for Zondervan to meet an urgent need in the marketplace, but as an opportunity for me to help John do for someone else what I was unable to do for Terry Furlow.

Julie Ackerman Link
Editor

INTRODUCTION

While writing this book, I picked up the September 23, 1986, issue of *USA Today*. A reporter had interviewed Dennis Hopper, the star of the 1960s film *Easy Rider*. Hopper claimed in the interview that members of the sixties drug culture were ". . . going to hold hands, take LSD, [and] find God. . . . We all ended up in total madness. . . ." I discussed the article with my wife, Bennie, and several others who knew about the book.

"Well, if you really think about it," Bennie explained, "all the people you describe in your book were looking for God."

"What do you mean?" I asked curiously.

"In the introductions to each chapter," she continued, "the people are all looking for something spiritual. Or at least something that could be described spiritually."

"I think you're sort of twisting this around," I answered. "Sure, it's a spiritual problem. I guess anything could be a spiritual problem."

She smiled and nodded in agreement. "Perhaps," she commented. "I'll make a note about what I mean and let you look at it."

Two days later she left this note, attached to the *USA Today* article, on my desk:

Chapter	Person	Spiritual Element
1	Caller	Love
2	Denny	Happiness (joy)
3	Walter	Peace of mind

4	Sandra	Acceptance, a form of love
5	Barry	A father to treat him kindly
6	Dan	Acceptance
7	Tom and family	Loyalty and agreement within the family
8	15 year old	Rapport/gentleness
9	Billy Lee Thompson	Control of his life

P.S. Read Galatians 5:22–23.

I found my Bible and began reading, "But the fruit of the Spirit is love, joy, peace, patience, kindness, goodness, faithfulness, gentleness, and self-control. Against such things there is no law." I read the passage again and began comparing it with the list Bennie had prepared. I reread Hopper's comments: "We were looking for God."

"I guess they were," I said to myself. "I guess we all are, in our own way." A lump formed in my throat. *Drugs, forbidden fruit. We're using drugs to replace what's missing in so many lives—the fruits of the Spirit.*

The deadliest enemies of nations are not their foreign foes. They always dwell within their own borders.

— William James

1

THE PROBLEM OF JUVENILE DRUG ABUSE

- How bad is the problem of drug abuse?
- What are the costs of drug abuse?
- Where did drug abuse start?
- How did the problem get so bad?

"It's not really drugs that's the problem, Doc," explained the caller. "Sure, drugs are what people see. But you take drugs for a reason. I took them because I was lonely. You can take the drugs away, but nobody ever told me how to take away the loneliness ..."

Something must occur after midnight that makes people more willing to be open about life. Or maybe it's just that people who call radio talk shows in the early morning hours are more open about themselves. This was my second visit to the Los Angeles area in four months. On each trip I had kept an almost frantic pace. In a three-day visit, I spoke at two conferences and participated in over a dozen radio and television interviews. The schedule was hectic, yet invigorating.

I had done this so often in the past year it was beginning to seem almost mechanical. At times, I wasn't even sure what city I was in. They all seem alike after

midnight. And through national and international
interviews I was learning that people are the same
throughout the world. We have the same problems, same
fears, and definitely the same loneliness. The caller
continued . . .

"Ya'll don't really understand," he pleaded in his deep
voice. "People take drugs because they're bothered about
something. They got problems. I mean I never met a
junkie who started out to be one! You don't start out
with that idea. That ain't nobody's goal. You take
something to get away from the pain and then it takes
you. The drink, the smoke, the coke, they become your
purpose for living. But they don't start out that way.

"Dig this, Doc. All I ever wanted was somebody to love
me; somebody I could talk to; somebody who cared. I
figured I'd never have that. With the junk, I don't worry
about it no more. The pain goes away.

"Tell the people to hear this. If they want to get rid of
drugs, they better focus on the problem. Drugs just ain't
the problem, man. Drugs is the crutch. Loneliness is the
problem. Drugs is a way of getting away from the
problem. That's what happened to Len Bias. Tell the
people that."

On June 17, 1986, Bias was probably the happiest young
man in the country. He had achieved his lifetime dream and
would be playing professional basketball with the Boston
Celtics. All-pro forward Larry Bird had declared he would
even attend rookie camp to get to play with Bias. A youngster's
dream was coming true.

But three days later Bias lay dead in a university apartment.
The world watched helplessly as the news media revealed the
nightmare. But the nightmare was not a dream.

Leonard Bias died of cocaine intoxication. This interrupted
normal electrical control of his heartbeat, which resulted in
sudden onset of seizures and cardiac arrest. The toxicological

study we did in addition to the cocaine analysis showed no alcohol or other drugs in his body at the time of death.

This terse statement by medical examiner Dr. John Smialek punctuated the career of one of the game's most exciting and emotion-filled basketball players and ended speculation about the death of Maryland athlete Len Bias. This tragic event inspired a new national focus on problems associated with drug abuse among the youth of our world. It was an incredible sacrifice.

Evidence indicated Bias was not a regular cocaine user. He had established a reputation for avoiding drug use but had been known to associate with friends who did use drugs, possibly on a regular basis. Apparently the peer pressure was stronger than Bias could tolerate, even at age twenty-two. Speculation is this could have been his first and only encounter with cocaine. Once was enough.

> *When you're doing the stuff you never think about O.D.ing. It's like, oh, sure, that happens to others, not me. I mean, I'll never die, you know? The thing is you become invincible while you're high.*
> *— Jennifer (age 15) Philadelphia*

During a stressful press conference following the medical examiner's report, Len Bias's former coach, Lefty Driesell, sent an emotional message to the world. "These are not recreational drugs," he sobbed. "They're killers."

Coach Driesell was stating a fact few people seem to realize. Drugs are killers. This certainly includes cocaine. *The American Heart Journal* recently published an article by one cardiologist who alone had attended seven separate cocaine-related deaths. These seven young people, age 20–37, had all used cocaine shortly before their apparent heart attacks.

Few people hear of these or the other approximately fifteen per week who suffer cocaine related deaths. Some people suggest that the problem would decrease if the deaths were more widely publicized. Apparently, that's a naive assumption. Only eight days after Bias's highly publicized tragic death another young athlete thought himself to be invincible. Professional football player Don Rogers ignored Bias's lesson and ended his life prematurely. Rogers, celebrating at his own bachelor party, died as a result of cocaine use.

His death also was widely reported, but again it didn't help. Three days later another young athlete was arrested on cocaine-related charges. He had just been drafted by the Cleveland Browns and would have been a teammate of Don Rogers.

How Bad Is the Problem of Drug Abuse?

The deaths and arrests of these athletes have reached public attention, but other harsh facts have not. In Los Angeles, five dollars will buy enough crack to cause severe addiction; crack-related emergency room admissions have increased over 500 percent in the past three years; and identified deaths by cocaine intoxication have tripled in the same period. Dr. Michael Walsh of the National Institute of Drug Abuse (NIDA) claims there were at least 700 cocaine-related deaths last year. Some authorities say his figure is vastly underestimated. Most cocaine-related deaths go unreported or are attributed to other causes. Similar to Bias's death, many are misdiagnosed as heart attacks.

According to NIDA, Americans now consume well over half the entire world's supply of illegal drugs. An estimated twenty million Americans smoke marijuana daily. Twenty-five million have experimented with cocaine. Possibly nine million of them are seriously addicted. Over one-half million people in this country are known to be heroin addicts. Some thirty million people take sedatives, and another twenty million take stimulants on a daily basis.

Eight million Americans chronically abuse tranquilizers. One hundred million consume alcohol regularly, and 15 percent of these are chronic alcoholics. Another sixty million smoke approximately two billion cigarettes per day. Over 120 million prescriptions are written annually for psychoactive drugs. All these are taken in addition to the three tons of aspirin we consume per day.

Studies show that in 1986 alone, 12 tons of heroin, 65 tons of marijuana, and 150 tons of cocaine were consumed throughout the United States. The sale of all these drugs hauled in over $100 billion, a figure that exceeds the net sales of General Motors. These numbers are only statistics, but those affected are people. And the youth of our country suffer most. Holly's story represents this as clearly as any.

As I sat in my office writing one Saturday evening, the telephone interrupted my concentration.

"Hello," I blurted.

"Is Dr. Baucom there?" The young voice whimpered.

"This is Dr. Baucom. This is John."

"Hey, John," she sighed. "This is Holly."

"What's wrong, Holly?" I asked.

"Momma's passed out on the floor. She's just laying there. Me and Sissy don't know what to do. A needle's hanging out of her arm. She's just laying there!"

I had been working with Holly's family in counseling for some time. Her mother, Irene, was a heroin addict and had been hospitalized for over two months. This was her first pass home.

"Where are you now, Holly?" I asked.

"In our new apartment," she stuttered. "What do we do?"

"I need to call the ambulance for your mom, Holly." I tried to sound calm. "What is your address?"

"I don't know! We're at Momma's new apartment. Nobody's here but us. Grandma's at her house and the phone's busy there—"

"Okay," I interrupted. "Let me hang up and I'll call you back within five minutes. What's your grandmother's telephone number? I'll get through."

I scribbled the number and then pushed the button to break our connection. I convinced an operator this was an emergency. She interrupted the grandmother's conversation and connected us. I informed Grandmother of the problem and told her to rush to Irene's apartment, which was only two blocks away. She gave me the address and I called for emergency medical help. Grandmother arrived moments before the ambulance.

Emergency medical personnel discovered Irene with the hypodermic needle still in her arm. She survived the trauma and returned to the drug treatment center several days later. Irene was discharged from the center after a few months more of treatment and is one of the few heroin addicts I have personally worked with who remained drug-free over any extended period of time.

That experience happened three years ago. As a sad postscript, I received a telephone call from Irene last month. Holly, now eighteen, was arrested earlier that day for prostitution. Apparently, she was earning money to support her own drug habit. Holly is now addicted to heroin.

> *You go out to the snow cone truck and this dude says—"Hey, I got another kind of snow that's better if you want it"—the dude's dealin' drugs, man. Sellin' coke to kids. It's sick.*
> *— Charlie (age 16) Charlotte*

In Columbia, South Carolina, police raided an ice cream vendor's office. The owner was arrested for selling cocaine from his Mr. Yummy ice cream trucks. In Philadelphia, a dentist was arrested for selling almost six million dollars' worth of cocaine per month, primarily to stockbrokers and lawyers. A few weeks later, in Houston, a seventy-five-year-old grandmother was arrested and later convicted of selling valium, codeine, and marijuana from her home. In Massachusets, Governor Michael Dukakis found in a 1984 survey that 60 percent of the state's high school students admitted having used illegal drugs on a regular basis. In San Jose, California, an undercover operation discovered 90 percent of some 400 employers of one Silicon Valley company were using drugs.

The drug epidemic is booming both nationwide and, indeed, worldwide. Its impact, unfortunately, is felt primarily by young people. Surveys reveal that 25 percent of high school students drink more than three beers per week. Forty percent of teenagers claim to smoke marijuana regularly. Seventy percent of high school students have tried marijuana. Alarmingly, only slightly over half of the adolescent population claim their parents have ever discussed drug use with them.

President Ronald Reagan described drugs as "the number one problem in our country." Other governmental leaders and national authorities echo similar beliefs. And well they might. National data indicates that the majority of teenagers have used alcohol and cigarettes. Another study reveals that over 90 percent of high school students will experiment with alcohol before they graduate and well over one-third will try marijuana. Seventeen percent will try cocaine. Ten percent will try LSD or some other hallucinogenic, and approximately 47 percent will use heroin before high school graduation. An additional research project by NIDA suggested 30 percent of all college students will try cocaine by their fourth year and over half will try marijuana. Eighty percent will experiment with some illegal drug by their mid-twenties.

What Are the Costs of Drug Abuse?

The cost of such abuse is staggering. The costs to industry alone from lost productivity, absenteeism, and accidents are conservatively estimated to be $47 billion per year. Drug abusers are three times as likely to be involved in industrial accidents; five times as likely to file worker's compensation claims; and use three times the sick benefits as non-drug users. An example of the cost was illustrated by one intoxicated employee in 1985. A mistake by a computer operator high on marijuana cost one airline $19 million. Similar statistics are found elsewhere in industry. Some are deadly. Since 1975 over fifty train accidents have been attributed to drug or alcohol impaired workers. This resulted in thirty-seven deaths and more than thirty-four million dollars' worth of destroyed property.

A former medical director of a company that assembles the space shuttle estimated that 20 to 25 percent of the employees in the plant were occasionally high on the job from alcohol or other drugs. Other experts estimate upwards of 23 percent of all U.S. workers use dangerous drugs on the job.

Health-care costs exceed those accrued by industry. One study suggested medical costs in the United States due to alcohol use alone exceed $116.7 billion per year. Cirrhosis of the liver, resulting almost exclusively from alcoholism, is now the fifth leading cause of death nationwide, surpassing even diabetes. Cirrhosis is the third leading cause of death for both men and women ages 25–65. If other forms of drug abuse are included, the costs soar to a staggering $170 billion annually. That figure is more than ten times higher than the government's budget allocated to fight drug abuse.

The cost of drug-related crimes has a major and immeasurable impact on other statistics. New York City Police Commissioner Benjamin Ward says crime is directly influenced by drugs. In fact, he states, "The crime problem in America today is the drug problem. . . ." In New York and Washington, a recent study revealed well over half the total criminal suspects tested were using drugs at the time of their arrest and 66 percent had used narcotics the day before their arrest. A University of Chicago study found alcohol and drug use to be directly related to the causes of theft and vandalism among all social levels. About 82 percent of these suspects admitted taking drugs. Over 30 percent of inmates in federal prisons are serving time because of drug-related arrests.

Drug abuse also takes a high toll from families. Alcoholics are more frequently separated and divorced than non-drinkers, and also more likely to be involved in family violence. In one study, well over half of the wife abusers in this country had drinking histories. Another report indicated nearly 70 percent of all child-abuse cases are alcohol related. Estimates indicate most rapes and 72 percent of criminal assaults are alcohol induced. Most studies of homicide indicate approximately 85 percent of all murderers and upwards of half the victims were drinking when the killing occurred.

The costs can also be measured in deaths. Although exact numbers are impossible to measure, evidence shows that more people will die from cocaine overdose in 1987 than from most medical illnesses. Add to this the number who die from causes indirectly related to cocaine use, such as accidents, and the total is staggering.

Over half of all traffic fatalities involve alcohol or some other drug. More significantly, drugs are involved in as many as 85 percent of pedestrian fatalities. Drugs and alcohol contribute to other kinds of accidents as well. Over 70 percent of all accidental deaths are drug related. Sixty-nine percent of all drownings involve drugs, as well as 63 percent of injuries resulting from falls. The statistics continue to build.

According to the National Association on Alcohol Abuse, over 100,000 Americans die each year from the effects of alcohol. This figure includes medical illness resulting from intoxication. But these figures seem small if viewed in comparison with America's favorite drug, nicotine. Despite the warnings and publicity given the anti-smoking campaign in the U.S., over 300,000 people die each year from tobacco-related deaths. According to the National Center for Health, almost 20 percent of the total deaths in the U.S. can be traced to cigarette smoking. Positive correlations have been found repeatedly in smoking and various diseases, including heart attack, atherosclerosis, lung cancer, bronchitis, and emphysema. Smoking kills over 52,000 Americans each year through chronic lung disease. Another 4,000 American lives are taken through cigarette-caused fires, and upwards of $30 billion per year are spent on health-care problems related to smoking. Similar costs are accumulated in Australia, Canada, Switzerland, and England. According to a July 1986 report in *USA*

Today, between 2 and 2.5 million lives are claimed world-wide, annually, due to tobacco addiction.

And the deaths continue. The damage continues. The pain continues. Why?

We are facing a crisis of gigantic proportions. One expert compared the problem to a worldwide forest fire burning out of control. Firemen are struggling unsuccessfully to extinguish the inferno. All their efforts, however, are not enough. They're armed only with squirt guns.

To understand how the fire grew to such proportions, we must look at the history of drug use in our country.

> *Well, it's no different than anything else.*
> *Everything is bad for you. Saccharin, sugar,*
> *coffee are all bad for you. Besides, cocaine is*
> *low-calorie.*
> —*Jessica (age 17) San Diego*

Where Did Drug Abuse Start?

Drug use is not new. Opium was apparently used by the Sumerians as early as 5000 B.C. Many South American Indians were chewing cocoa leaves, the source of cocaine, at approximately the same time. The Chinese distilled alcohol as early as 2000 B.C. American Aztec Indians took ololiuqui, a natural substance similar in structure to the compound we know as LSD, during their religious rites.

When our own Puritan forefathers lifted anchor to sail to the New World, they left with 42 tons of beer and 10,000 tons of wine, but only 4 tons of water. Apparently they considered alcohol more important than water. In fact, the term we use today to measure alcohol content originated from these ancestors. The expression originated when gunpowder moistened by alcoholic beverages was lighted. If it exploded, it was "proof" the beverage contained an adequate amount of alcohol. The term is still in use, though the test is not.

Four generations later Chief Sitting Bull reportedly mixed

marijuana with tobacco and passed the peace pipe. The soldiers by then had apparently already been exposed to marijuana. Various kinds of tobacco were chewed during colonial times, and after 1810 smoking it became common. During and after the Civil War, wounded soldiers were treated with narcotics. The recently discovered hypodermic syringe made it so easy to administer these pain-relieving drugs that many soldiers became addicted. For some time addiction was called the "army disease." At approximately the same time, opium smoking for pleasure began in our country. Chinese workers imported to help construct the railroads brought opium with them. From railroad workers the practice spread to the underworld.

How Did the Problem Get So Bad?

Physicians continued to generously prescribe morphine for various complaints and allowed prescriptions to be filled repeatedly. Others medicated themselves with over-the-counter potions containing morphine, heroin, or cocaine. In fact, cocaine received widespread consumption as an ingredient in Coca-Cola until early in this century. As a result, by the early 1900s over ninety-seven million Americans were addicted. Finally, in 1914 the government passed legislation to control the manufacture, sale, and use of opiates and cocaine. When drugs became illegal, millions of addicts resorted to illegal measures to continue their habit.

Alcohol use continued to increase along with public opposition to it. In the late 1800s several states passed laws prohibiting its use. By the end of World War I over half the states were legislated as "dry." In 1920 the Eighteenth Amendment became law and prohibited the sale of alcohol. Most historians agree that Prohibition failed to eliminate drinking. In fact, some claim drinking increased during this era. It certainly transformed the culture of drinking and created a new language. Terms such as speakeasy, bootlegger, bathtub gin, wets and drys became common. Prohibition also made many illegal entrepreneurs incredibly wealthy.

By the 1930s it became evident that the law was unenforce-able. Prohibition had become a joke. People simply ignored the law. In 1933 it was repealed. Drinking had increased during Prohibition, but it increased even more after the repeal. It became respectable and socially valuable. Those who used liquor looked down on those who did not, not unlike today.

Drug use today, and almost all alcohol use, is not only accepted but seen as a rite of passage into adulthood. Adolescents, especially young males, see it as a socially acceptable way of expressing their maturity. The use of drugs other than alcohol is increasing slowly among teenagers. Alcohol use, however, is growing almost exponentially. Along with this increase is the continued upward spiral of sobering statistics.

I left the radio studio in a somber mood. A number of calls had been stimulated by the news of Len Bias's death. The reports were still sketchy but rumors indicated cocaine was involved. I didn't want to believe it. Neither did any athlete or serious fan of basketball. Len Bias was one in a million. Many had described him as perhaps the finest basketball player ever to compete on the collegiate level. The ink wasn't even dry on his multi-million-dollar contract. And it all meant nothing.

He was dead.

The calls had been disturbing. The news hurt as only the truth can. My motel was less than a mile away, so I decided to walk back. I needed time to think. My mind kept going back to the most memorable call. The deep bass voice haunted me. There was such sincerity in what he said.

"You can take the drugs away, but nobody ever told me how to take away the loneliness . . . All I ever wanted was somebody to love me . . . Drugs just ain't the problem, man. Loneliness is the problem. . . ."

I kept hearing his voice and the silence following his call. I had no easy answer to give, no witty response, and no comfort to offer. He had hit all of us between the eyes with his street-wise explanation.

But somebody has to take a step, I thought. The best place to start is probably with the basic unit of society, the family. If someone can get to parents and let them know the truth about the problem . . .

I looked at my watch. It was 1:45 A.M. Almost 5:00 A.M. back home, I thought. I wasn't too tired; besides, if I was in Chattanooga I'd be getting up in an hour.

From the southern California deserts a warm Santa Ana wind blew in, casting a spell over the early morning street still crowded with cars. I saw an empty bench in front of my motel and sat down to think. I inhaled the clean, warm desert air and opened my valise. Inside was my usual supply of 3 x 5 cards. I pulled one out and began to scribble an outline.

"Number 1," I said aloud. "The Problem of Juvenile Drug Abuse. Number 2, The Drugs Juveniles Abuse . . ."

I looked up, thinking what to write next. A star arched across the sky, leaving a bright sparkling trail behind. It dropped in peaceful slow motion, dunking beneath the horizon. Gone. "Number 3, . . ."

Questions for Inquiry

1. What new insights do you have concerning the magnitude of the drug problem after reading chapter 1?
2. What is now more obvious to you about the presence of the drug problem within your community, your social network, your family?
3. How did you respond to the statistics in this chapter regarding the extent of teen involvement with drugs (i.e., the percentage of students who abuse drugs and those predicted to do so before graduation)? How will these statistics change your behavior or consumption of "drugs"?
4. Are you willing to admit that your children may become involved with drugs? If not, why do you think they are immune?
5. In what ways are you and your family affected by the costs or damages of drug abuse?

Family or Group Activity

Begin family discussion sessions on areas related to the problem of juvenile drug abuse as presented in each chapter of this book. Explore each family member's awareness, information, or lack of information. Spend time helping to correct misinformation.

Journal Entry

To demonstrate to yourself how difficult it is to abstain from using drugs, try the following. For the period of time it takes you to read this book, stop using one of the following items: caffeine, cigarettes, alcohol, chocolate, or sugar. Keep notes in a personal journal or notebook. Record daily what you feel physiologically, psychologically, socially, etc. Be as open as you feel comfortable. The journal is for your private use.

For Further Thought

Why do you think churches have not had a more significant impact on the drug problem than they have? How could your church be more actively involved in solving the drug problem?

What is dangerous about the tranquilizers is that whatever peace of mind they bring is a packaged peace of mind. Where you buy a pill and buy peace with it, you get conditioned to cheap solutions instead of deep ones.
— Max Lerner, *"The Assault on the Mind,"*
The Unfinished Country *(1959)*

2

THE DRUGS JUVENILES ABUSE

- What is a drug?
- Does one kind of drug use lead to another?
- What drugs are juveniles abusing?

The ringing doorbell interrupted my concentration. Looking through the door I recognized the face of a former student from my days as a college teacher. It had been at least six years since we'd seen each other, but his appearance had changed little.

"Put on a little weight, haven't you?" he teased.

"Thanks a lot, Gene," I responded. "By the way, what grade did I give you?" We both laughed. It was good to see each other and we caught up on the past years and reminisced over mutual friends and memories.

"You knew Danny got killed, didn't you?" he finally asked.

"Yeah. I heard it was a car wreck. Pretty gruesome, huh?"

"What a guy," Gene recalled. "He had everything going for him. Girls, money, brains. He never had to study, never had to look for a date, nothing. He never realized how good he had it. You knew he was a junkie, didn't you?"

"No. I'd heard different things, but I didn't know anything for sure."

"That's hard to believe," Gene responded. "All the students knew about it. The guy was a walking pharmacy. You could buy anything from him. It was funny because he was a pre-med student, a behavioral science major, wasn't he?"

"Yeah, I guess he was," I answered with a degree of guilt. "I wasn't his advisor or anything, but he was a major."

"He liked you a lot," Gene commented thoughtfully. "He thought you were a great teacher. Said you seemed to care."

"Really? He wasn't even in one of my classes, was he?"

"Don't you remember? He was in the Psych of Adjustment class. I was your reader for that class. Yeah, he was in there. On 'deviant day' he dressed up like a pimp. Don't you remember?"

Memories finally began to surface. I recalled conversations I had had with Danny many years earlier. "Yes," I answered. "Now I remember. I remember several things. Maybe I missed something. Maybe I missed an opportunity to help him."

Gene stared at me blankly. "Not just you. We all did."

> Yeah, well anyway, we went on a run and did some dope and did too much I guess, or something. But you know, I passed out and the cops found me. I stayed a couple of days in intensive care, but I'm all right. . . . Probably do it again someday. It doesn't bother me.
>
> — Charlie (age 14) Phoenix

Most parents are painfully undereducated as to the problem of drug abuse. This includes both the big picture of how the problem affects society and the smaller picture of how the drugs actually affect our children. (See Appendix A—Drug Awareness Chart.) Even those who are professionally trained to deal with the problem can be woefully naive. Educating ourselves about juvenile drug abuse must be an ongoing process. The drug subculture changes so rapidly we must constantly update our understanding of language, customs, and trends. For example, most authorities agree that cocaine is now easier to purchase and more frequently abused than marijuana. Yet, that trend has only occurred very recently, and it reverses a trend of several years. Similarly, the names of drugs change rapidly with both time and location. Cocaine can be called coke, rock, crack, base, or snow, depending on where you are and to whom you're talking. (See Appendix B— Glossary.) The discussion in this chapter is devoted to factors common to basic drug awareness.

No amount of knowledge, however, can substitute for simple "plain vanilla" attentiveness. Paying attention can make up for lack of knowledge.

What Is a Drug?

In this book alcohol is included among the list of substances known as drugs. *A drug is a habit-forming substance that directly affects the brain and nervous system and changes mood, perception, or consciousness.* This definition includes many substances, some legal, and others illegal. No one can adequately explain why moderate use of alcohol and tobacco are generally accepted by our society though both are directly responsible for far more deaths than heroin, cocaine, or marijuana, which are clearly illegal and frowned on. On the other hand, tobacco does not craze people to the extent that they will kill or rob to purchase it. There are hundreds of cases where people have killed to buy cocaine, heroin, or marijuana.

Just because a drug is legal does not mean it is harmless. Over thirty million pounds of aspirin are consumed each year in our country. Aspirin, however, can cause gastrointestinal bleeding, ulcers, and other ailments. Similarly, prescription drugs can be addictive. Yet, according to a 1980 report by the U.S. Bureau of Census, over four million drug prescriptions are filled per day in this country. Daily, over $30 million of prescription drugs are purchased in the United States. We are indeed a drug culture.

> *I was six the first time I did any drugs. I wanted to be like my big brother. . . . He was ten and dealing. . . . I started with marijuana and then did speed, coke, and ludes. It was cool.*
> *— Tony (age 11) Memphis*

Does One Kind of Drug Use Lead to Another?

The evolutionary aspects of drug use are real. There is, beyond any doubt, a predictable progression to drug use. Children almost never experiment with cocaine, heroin, or any of the "hard" drugs without first using gateway drugs: marijuana, alcohol, and/or tobacco. Two studies found a constant progression of drug use among high school students. The pattern consistently followed four well-defined steps.

1. beer or wine.
2. hard liquor and/or cigarettes.
3. marijuana.
4. other illicit drugs.

Researchers reported that virtually no one moves to step four without first going through steps one, two, and three. A sampling of New York college students supported the other research. In this study, 99 percent of people who used illegal drugs regularly had started with tobacco and then marijuana. An interview with a man I had met in counseling illustrated this fact.

"Why me?" Robin asked. "Why did I do drugs? Everybody did where I grew up. That's just the way it was. And everybody became junkies or heads or dopers. The others became cops. Yeah, you was either a junkie or a cop."

Robin stared at me. His eyes still seemed glazed and distant. At the time of our interview he had been drug free for three months. He wore his thirty-eight years roughly—he appeared to be at least fifteen years older. Robin claimed to have followed the typical progression of drug abuse.

"Well yeah, I did it all. Started smoking cigarettes when I was in the first grade. Weed the same year. Drank hard liquor by the time I was ten or eleven. More weed. I loved weed. I used to bake the best brownies with that stuff. You'd like them. . . . Heroin was like discovering sex or something for the first time. It is the ultimate tranquilizer. My entire body would have an orgasm all at once. I was a fiend man, a real dope fiend back in those days."

"Why did you decide to quit?" I asked.

His dark, hollow eyes fixed on the ceiling as he thought about how to answer. I noticed how unusually thin he was. His pale skin appeared to be stretched tightly around his jaw. Finally, snapping his head back, he turned toward me.

"You become a slave to it. You lose yourself to the dope. It becomes your god, your wife, your purpose, your lover, everything all rolled into one. The only thing in my life was my skag. I'd kill for it. If I thought you was going to take my fix, I would have wiped you out—even if you was my best friend, or my daddy. It didn't mean nothin' . . .

"Can I quit? So far I have. But the needle talks to you. It's sweet. It'll call your name. 'Say, come here sugar.' You score, fix, and puke. It's beautiful. Whew! It's going to be tough man, I know that. But I've got a chance now. I want to be my own man. I'm too old and tired for hustlin'. I miss the high, but I don't miss the price you pay for it. And I don't mean money. I don't want to belong to heroin no more."

Life's a drag and then you die. . . . That's it.
That's all I've got to say.
— Carla (age 14) Ashville

What Drugs Are Juveniles Abusing?

The first drugs abused by most children are alcohol or tobacco. Since the early 1960s when the anti-smoking campaign began, tobacco consumption has increased by 70 percent. The sharpest increase is registered among adolescents. Well over 50 percent of adolescents will attempt smoking by age eighteen. In one study over 40 percent of adolescent boys reported themselves as "regular smokers" by age seventeen.

The psychologically addictive quality of tobacco is substantial. The smoking habit is extremely difficult to break. A public and historic example is the father of psychiatry, Sigmund Freud. Although aware that his twenty-cigar-per-day habit was destroying his health he continued to smoke. Even after his cancerous jaw was removed, Freud continued the destructive habit. He tried various times to quit, but he was helpless over his habit, as thousands of others have been. Finally, in 1934, after cancer had eaten through his cheek, Freud died.

The danger of tobacco is also its "gateway" effect. Most teenagers who smoke marijuana or use harder drugs, began with cigarettes. Incidentally, this was also true with Freud, who was a notorious user of cocaine in his later years.

> *Yeah, I do weed. I like myself better when I smoke. I laugh a lot. . . . No I don't think it'll hurt me—Why? Do you?*
> — *Curt (age 20) Atlanta*

Marijuana is known as grass, pot, weed, and joint. It comes from the hemp plant, which grows throughout the world. Fibers from the hemp plant can be used to produce rope, paper, and clothing. But its primary usage comes from the leaf that forms marijuana and its resin that forms hashish. Both can be eaten, but are usually dried and smoked in rolling papers. The effects of both drugs vary according to the user. Various emotions can be produced as well as talkativeness, hilarity, or dizziness. Increased relaxation and self-confidence can also result from short-term marijuana use.

The active element in both marijuana and hashish is THC (deta 9 tetrahydrocannabinol), a chemical that can store itself in fatty tissue. As a result it can accumulate in the body and cause a reverse tolerance. As the smoker's THC level rises, it takes less of the substance to produce the "high" effect. Long-term marijuana users require less of the drug to become intoxicated. An ongoing debate as to the adverse effects of long-term marijuana use has not yet settled the issue. However, at least four possibilities exist.

The first problem with long-term abuse is that marijuana appears to be a stepping stone drug. Not all marijuana users progress to heroin, but 99 percent of heroin users began their drug habit with marijuana. That issue has been scientifically resolved. The second possible adverse effect has to do with long-term use in men. There is sufficient evidence to prove that marijuana reduces the level of the male hormone, testosterone. This can result in impaired sexual activity and loss of interest in sexual relationships. A similar effect may occur in women and lead to infertility. Third, evidence shows that marijuana abuse can affect the body's disease-fighting capacity. This immune system damage is measurable, but the long-term impact is yet to be established. The final problem is one of impaired judgment, short-term memory loss, apathy, and general lack of drive. It is a well-accepted clinical fact that this "amotivated syndrome" is often found in chronic marijuana abusers of all ages. Alarmingly, it is most notable in teenagers.

The symptoms of marijuana use include altered perceptions, red eyes, dry mouth, reduced concentration, euphoria, laughing, and hunger. Evidence of marijuana use includes rolling papers, pipes, dried material, odor of burnt rope, and metal clips (roach clips).

> *It's sexy. No odor, no smoke, don't have to get messy. It helped me lose weight, too. It is very feminine. And what a rush!*
> *— Tanya (age 19) Birmingham*

Cocaine is obtained from the leaves of the South American cocoa plant. It is also known as coke, snow, rock, base, and in its most powerful form, crack. Ten years ago it was considered non-addicting and relatively harmless. Today, it is the fastest-growing drug problem among the entire population. More than one out of ten Americans has tried it and roughly 5,000 people try it for the first time each day. There are at least five million addicted cocaine users, and over one-third of all college students will try it before they graduate. The death of Len Bias dramatically illustrates that cocaine can indeed kill, even on the first try. Even a small amount can cause a heart attack, seizure, or stroke.

Cocaine is generally absorbed into the nasal membranes by sniffing. It may also be injected or chewed by the leaf. It constricts the blood vessels and tissues, leading to increased strength and endurance. Some users experience a feeling of euphoria, excitement, restlessness, suspiciousness, and energy. One frightening side effect of chronic cocaine use is the illusion of bugs crawling on the skin. This can often lead to confusion and possible physical damage as the user tries to rid himself of the imaginary bugs.

According to the NIDA, anyone who uses cocaine regularly over extended periods of time will become addicted. Cocaine use has spread through every element of American society. Nearly 20 percent of high school students try cocaine, and close to 8 percent of high school seniors use it daily. Dr. Mark Goldman of the cocaine help-line (1-800-COCAINE) receives approximately 1,200 calls per day. In a recent survey of teenage callers he found 79 percent were absent from school regularly; 71 percent reported substantially reduced grades; 59 percent reported being high while at school; 48 percent were "dealing" (selling drugs) in school to support their habits; 39 percent stole from family and friends to support their habit; 89 percent admitted problems with their families were directly attributable to cocaine; and 37 percent believed suicide was the only cure for their addiction.

A new form of cocaine is crack. A pea-shaped crystalline

ball made by boiling cocaine, crack is smoked or inhaled. A single dose of crack costs five to ten dollars, whereas a gram of cocaine costs about 100 dollars. Crack is probably the most addictive drug available today. A person can become enslaved to it from just one experience. Once addicted, the side effects include deep depression and severe paranoia. The euphoria crack gives can occur in seven seconds, a very rapid response time, and lasts usually ten minutes or less. The "high" is reportedly far more powerful and seductive than any other known drug. This adds to the drug's addictive nature.

Crack and cocaine use can result in memory problems, paranoia, perforated nasal passages, lung tissue damage, high blood pressure, brain seizure, heart attack, and stroke. Evidence of cocaine use includes glass vials, glass pipes, white crystalline powder, razor blades, syringes, and needle marks.

> *It was like a fog slowly lifting from my eyes and as I looked up, there was this police officer. He looked like God, man. But he was a brother—he was black! And I thought his badge was the button to end the world. But I was confused because I didn't know God was a brother. So I asked him about it and he thought I was smartin' off. I never told him I was on acid.*
>
> *—Dale (age 23) Dalton*

Hallucinogens are a class of drugs that distort the user's sensory perceptions. Popularly called "psychedelics" in the late 1960s, they create hallucinations of sights and sounds that do not exist in external reality. According to a federal government report one American out of twenty has tried a hallucinogen at least once. Hallucinogens include mescaline, psilocyben, PCP, and LSD. By far the most popular drug of this type is LSD.

LSD was the center of research activity in the late fifties and early sixties. The drug was so powerful that even some researchers became strongly addicted to it. Even today, it is the most frequently used drug of its class. LSD is derived from a fungus that grows on rye and other plants and is extremely potent. A single ounce of LSD can produce 300,000 doses. It is consumed orally, usually in a sugar cube. The effects vary individually. Some people have reported seeing sounds and hearing colors. Others have a complex distortion of shapes and sizes. An LSD "trip" can last up to eighteen hours and can be terrifying. Some people have reported very traumatic experiences resulting in complete loss of contact with reality. Others have reported totally peaceful and pleasant states. The reaction is unpredictable.

Phencyclidine PCP (also known as angel dust) is actually used legally to tranquilize elephants and has effects similar to LSD. More often, however, it results in violence and disassociation. Other side effects include anxiety, panic, and nausea. When mixed with alcohol, PCP predictably results in violent behavior. As with LSD, PCP can be found in capsules, tablets, sugar cubes, or blotter squares. It can also be smoked after being sprinkled in a marijuana cigarette. Evidence of ingestion includes altered mood, altered perceptions, an acute focus on detail, and a distorted sense of reality. It is a dangerous drug and leads to the inability to think clearly. Long-term use can lead to severe emotional dysfunction. Physical symptoms include increased heart rate, hyperactivity, goose bumps, increased sweating, and dilated pupils. There is also a chance of flashbacks (recurrences) long after the dose was taken. Many people have been hospitalized for emotional disorders on a long-term basis from chronic abuse of hallucinogens.

> *I started out shooting in my arms. When I couldn't find a vein I went between my toes. Eventually, right in here—under my tongue— yeah! You run out of veins after a while. Hepatitis caught up with me but I didn't quit. Most junkies just grow old and get on maintenance. Yeah, methadone.*
> *—Domino (age 41) Chicago*

Narcotics are a group of drugs that induce relaxation. In fact, narcotic means "sleep-inducing." Yet most narcotics today are used to elicit euphoric feelings. The narcotics include opium, derivatives of opium, and synthetic drugs that duplicate the effects of opium. The opium poppy grows legally in many countries, including Turkey, Pakistan, Southeast Asia, and Colombia. The drug is a dried form of the liquid substance extracted from the seed pods after sprouting.

Morphine was isolated as one of the most powerful ingredients of opium in the early nineteenth century. It was soon used widely as a pain reliever and became available both in prescription and non-prescription forms. After thousands of users were already hooked, scientific studies concluded how highly addictive morphine actually was. In 1875 researchers discovered they could create heroin by causing various minor chemical changes in morphine. They claimed the new miracle drug was far stronger than morphine and non-addictive. History has proved them woefully wrong.

Heroin abuse has stabilized at half a million users. It is normally taken by injection beneath the skin or directly into a vein. The "rush" is very intense and preceded by a brief period of nausea. Some have described the rush as similar to a sexual experience and very addicting. Tolerance to this drug comes rapidly, so increased dosages are required to reach the same euphoria. The drug is unavailable legally and very expensive. Most users resort to crime to support their expensive habit.

Part of the addicting effect of the drug is the gripping pain of withdrawal. Symptoms begin some six hours after injection and are extremely unpleasant. Symptoms include chills, cramps, sweating, nervousness, runny nose, hot and cold flashes, diarrhea, nausea, headache, hallucinations, and craving for more of the drug. As severe as these symptoms sound, few people have actually died from withdrawal. Yet, few addicts ever recover from the addiction.

Physical symptoms of heroin use include euphoria, insensitivity to pain, nausea, and watery eyes. Evidence of heroin use includes needle marks (usually on the forearms), syringes, spoons, cold skin, and frequent wearing of long sleeve shirts, even in excessive heat, to hide the needle marks or "tracks." The dangers of long-term addiction include personality deterioration, loss of interest in work, malnutrition, blood poisoning, hepatitis, and death. A further danger is the possibility of contracting AIDS from the syringe.

> After huffing you get this buzz on, see. You get the buzz, places you ain't supposed to. I mean you see the buzz! It's like lightning sticking out in front of you. You get the buzz all over. Then you get sick. But you try it again.
> — David (age 16) Pensacola

Substances such as model airplane glue, industrial glues, gasoline, paint thinner, and other solvents can be abused as inhalants. These substances are legal, but can be used for the same purposes as the more highly publicized illegal drugs. As the name implies, the fumes from these chemicals are inhaled, often from a paper bag or rag. They produce euphoria, dizziness, loss of coordination, slurred speech, and occasional delusions. This is followed by a period of dizziness or stupor, after which the user may have amnesia of the event.

Evidence of inhalant abuse includes the odor of the substance, poor muscle control, reported headaches, sneezing, chest pains, drowsiness, and intoxication. The dangers of inhalant abuse are quite serious. Side effects range from unconsciousness to pulmonary injury, brain damage, or sudden death.

> No, not me, but I had some friends who were speed freaks. These people are idiots. It makes them paranoid. Makes them crazy. It's like something from some horror movie or something. A guy takes speed like that he's going to end up dead or in the funny farm. That's what I think about it.
> — Tom (age 17) San Diego

The class of drugs known as stimulants include amphetamines, other stimulants, and even caffeine. They act by stimulating the central nervous system. As any long-term user of caffeine who has tried to quit knows, it is addictive. Caffeine can cause insomnia, restlessness, and gastrointestinal irritation. However, it has few other known adverse side effects.

Amphetamines are synthetic drugs. They act as caffeine does, but far more powerfully and far more dangerously. They can be medicinally used if prescribed and monitored by a physician. Problems arise from unmonitored higher doses and continual use over an extended period. The epitomy of amphetamine addiction is the "speed freak" who injects a liquid "upper" into his veins and remains awake for a three- to four-day period. This often leads to paranoid and violent behavior that closely resembles the symptoms of paranoid schizophrenia. In fact, speculation exists that paranoid schizophrenia is caused by the same chemical changes in the brain as those induced artificially by amphetamines.

Amphetamines are usually taken orally in tablet or capsule form, but can also be injected. An overdose can cause coma, brain damage, and death. Other dangers include hepatitis, hallucinations, and severe emotional disturbance. Amphetamine highs are normally followed by severe depression. Long-term abuse often results in hospitalization. Symptoms of amphetamine or other stimulant use include alertness, talkativeness, appetite loss, and mood elevation. Evidence of use includes the presence of pills and capsules, loss of sleep, irritability, weight loss, and hyperactivity.

> *My boyfriend got me started. It was glorious. I tell ya'. I would drop a red and float through class. Nobody even knew it! There was no smell or nothin'. I could spend my lunch money on a red and mellow out.*
> — *Janie (age 16) Greensboro*

Depressants include barbiturates, sedatives, tranquilizers, and other drugs that act to relax the central nervous system.

Alcohol is also a depressant, but is covered more completely in the next chapter. Other than alcohol, barbiturates are the most common form of depressant and are derived from barbituric acid. Enough barbiturates are manufactured annually in this country to provide forty doses for every man, woman, and child. They are prescribed by physicians legally and also widely sold illegally.

Depressants cause effects similar to alcohol. They relax the user and remove inhibitions, increase drowsiness, and reduce coordination. Prolonged use can cause physical dependence. Tranquilizers, such as valium, reduce anxiety. They too are extremely addictive and dangerous. The extent of tranquilizer use is noted by the National Institute of Drug Abuse, which reports that 100 million prescriptions are written each year.

Many authorities consider tranquilizer and barbiturate addiction to be the most severe, dangerous, and resistant to treatment. Abrupt withdrawal can cause convulsions, seizures, and death. Other than alcohol and tobacco, the highest number of drug-related deaths result from barbiturates. Barbiturates, often used in combination with alcohol, are the drug of choice for suicide attempts. Physical symptoms of barbiturate use are depressed breathing, intoxication, and drowsiness. Evidence of use includes the presence of capsules or pills, confused behavior, extensive sleep, and slurred speech. Clear dangers include accidental overdose, muscle rigidity, and severe addiction.

> *Designers are really the drug of the future. It's like the Calvin Klein of highs—elite. I took my first hit of ecstasy in Aspen—poetry isn't it?— ecstasy in Aspen!*
>   *—Brenda (age 20) Denver*

Two drug phenomena, polydrug abuse and designer drugs, have not been discussed. Polydrug abuse is abuse of more than one drug at a time, or several drugs over a period of time. This process is becoming more widespread and common. It is extremely dangerous and can result in far more complex addictions. It also increases the dangers from overdose.

The most recent trend is toward what are being called "designer drugs." This unfortunate and misleading label has endowed the drug with a seductive, prestigious status. Authorities fear these drugs will constitute the next epidemic. Designer drugs are synthetic combinations of available substances into one capsule. This combination produces the effects, as an example, of a stimulant combined with a hallucinogen. Designers are extremely powerful and equally dangerous. Fenatyl, a designer substance, is a synthetic duplicate of heroin, but it can be a thousand times stronger than heroin. Designers are difficult to detect, other than by observable changes in behavior. Several hundred people have been killed by the drugs and others permanently disabled with symptoms like Parkinson's disease.

Awareness of these adverse side effects unfortunately does not deter further drug use. The epidemic rages, regardless of deaths. Increasing as well is the availability of high technology to manufacture new drugs. Computers are used to create newer and more powerful drugs, customized to create "made-to-order" highs. As one drug's dangerous side effects are discovered, a new and more potent analog is being manufactured. This is indeed warfare. And the "good guys" are losing.

Maybe I missed it. Like on so many other occasions I was distracted or I didn't notice. Perhaps, I just didn't care enough to pay attention. It's easy to miss things. In a case like this it's also easy to get locked into the "if onlys." "If only I'd intervened maybe Danny would be alive today . . . If only I'd reached out more . . ."

I had repressed my memories of Danny, primarily because I didn't understand his death. Before my visit with Gene, it had been years since I had even thought about Danny. One conversation we shared, however, now stood out clearly. We sat in my small office ostensibly to discuss his final grade. Instead, we talked about other things, including his dreams and goals. Danny had a reputation for being a rabble rouser on campus. I had a similar reputation among the faculty. Perhaps this was why he sought me out.

"What do you want, Danny?" I asked. "What are you looking for?"

He looked out the window and fixed his eyes on two children rolling down the grassy hill, laughing. He held his hands together, forefingers peaking to a pyramid and tapping together rhythmically.

"That." He nodded. "I want that kind of freedom, happiness, joy."

"Right," I laughed. "Let me know where you find it. I'd like it myself."

He quit smiling and his face became very serious. He leaned over and spoke softly. "It's out there somewhere. Someday I'll find it. And if I do, I'll sell you some."

I spoke to Danny about happiness being internal instead of external. Looking back though, maybe he was sending a message that I simply wasn't receiving. If I had heard and responded to him differently, perhaps I could have helped him find what he was seeking. He didn't find it in drugs.

Gene had stimulated my thinking. It took me several days to get all the information. Danny had died in 1983, but not from an automobile accident. The car he was in did wreck. Danny was declared dead, however, from a barbiturate overdose. Apparently, he died at the wheel and the car left the highway. Nobody else was injured.

What a waste. Whatever he was seeking was elusive. I don't think he found it.

Questions for Inquiry

1. What did you read in this chapter that was new, surprising, or alarming?
2. Are you aware of any suspicious signs or symptoms displayed by your child or any other juvenile that you know?
3. What prescribed medications or legal drugs (i.e., nicotine, alcohol, aspirin, etc.) are available in your home? Take an inventory of any current or outdated or forgotten medications lying around. What does the presence of these drugs communicate to you or others?
4. Have you noticed any behavior or personality changes in your child that may be related to drug abuse?
5. What is your understanding of the progressive use of drugs, i.e., legal drugs preceding the use of more malignant ones?

Family or Group Activity

Research the extent of the juvenile drug-abuse problem in your community. Discuss with teachers, police officers, and youth counselors what drugs are being abused, sources of drugs, and where and when purchases are occurring. Continue family discussions and share your information. Ask juveniles if the data is accurate. Support any and all attempts to avoid involvement with drug abuse and share information with juveniles on how to do this.

Journal Entry

Make a list of all drugs you have used in the past year. Include prescription drugs, over-the-counter drugs, and any illegal drugs. Do you feel that you have become overly dependent on any?

Comment also on your responses to abstaining from whatever substance you have chosen. How has your experience affected your concern and/or empathy with those who may be "hooked" on drugs? If you haven't begun to abstain from any drug, begin at this point.

For Further Thought

Would you be willing to discuss with your teenager how you feel about abstaining from the "drug" you have become dependent on? Are you willing to admit the power it has had over you? If not, why?

Put a man in a room where he can play dominoes, read newspapers, and have what he considers good talk, and you will observe that he will not drink as fast or as deep, or as strongly as he otherwise would. In short there would be other things to amuse him besides drinking; and what does he drink for, but to amuse himself, and to forget troubles of every kind?
— *Sir Arthur Helps*, Organization in Daily Life

3

THE DRUG OF CHOICE

- What is the history of alcohol abuse in the U.S.?
- How widespread is the problem of alcohol abuse today?
- What types of teenagers are most likely to abuse alcohol?
- What is an alcoholic?
- What are the symptoms of alcohol addiction?
- What are the stages of alcohol addiction?

When I met Walter he was a very likeable nineteen year old who had been using drugs since he was twelve. Walter entered counseling as a result of a "bad trip" suffered from a high dose of PCP, a powerful hallucinogen. During this particular trip he "blacked out." Though awake, conscious, and ambulatory, he was totally unaware of anything going on around him.

In Walter's drugged mind, he was trapped inside a huge trash dumpster and couldn't get out. In reality, he was inside a men's restroom at a local restaurant. But reality did not agree with Walter's intoxicated perceptions. Attempting to beat his way out of the dumpster he scratched the brick walls of the restroom until he suffered bone-deep cuts on his fists and all his fingers. He demolished the sink, toilet bowl, light fixtures, and paper towel dispenser.

Three men in the bathroom were injured, one severely, and when the police officers arrived, Walter bit one so deeply the officer required surgery. The other officers realized it was probably a case of PCP intoxication and called an animal control officer. The "dog catcher" brought a large mesh net used to capture runaway zoo animals, and Walter was subsequently apprehended. He was neither injured nor killed, which showed the incredible restraint and professionalism of the police officers. When he finally regained consciousness thirty-six hours later, he was bandaged, sewn up, and in jail. He had absolutely no memory of the events.

When sober, Walter was the most likeable young man you could ever meet. He was sincere, dependable, and seemed to seriously want to work on his problem. He agreed to try not using drugs during the course of counseling. He had been abstaining for five weeks before I discovered I was not paying close enough attention.

"Oh," he explained during one session. "It's no big deal. I like it okay without drugs. My friends seem to understand. Since I got busted and everything, nobody pushes me to do anything. They just sort of let me alone. I mean they offer me a hit now and then, but I say no and they understand, I guess." Walter gestured with his bandaged hands. He was facing several charges from his arrest and quite a large fine for damages.

"Aren't you tempted to use anything now?" I asked. "It's unusual for somebody to just go cold-turkey without any problem. You've been hooked for a long time."

"No. I get sick and stuff, but that's because I'm not used to drinking so much. But other than that, I'm fine."

I sat in stunned silence for a moment, hoping I had not heard correctly. "Drinking." I finally spoke. "You mean booze?"

"Yeah, I've been drinking since you asked me to try being drug free! Not a lot, really. Probably a six pack and a pint a night. It really makes me sick . . ."

"Walter," I interrupted. "Alcohol isn't a drug to you, is it?"

"No," he sounded surprised. "Booze isn't a drug. A drug is like cocaine, marijuana, 'ludes, angel dust, and stuff like that. Booze isn't a drug. Is it?"

"Walter, we need to talk."

In my enthusiasm to rescue Walter, I had been blinded to the reality. I had not paid attention. To Walter, like a lot of other people, being drug free had nothing to do with his consumption of alcohol.

What Is the History of Alcohol Abuse in the U.S.?

Throughout the history of our country, Americans have had a love-hate relationship with alcohol. The beverage has held significance in religious rituals, medical practice, and dietary use. On the other hand, it has simultaneously been scourged as demonic and evil. In the early history of our country it was a routine part of everyday life, but those found drunk were placed in stocks for public display and ridicule. Public taverns were not only encouraged, but in some areas required by law. Even with early pilgrim settlers, the paradoxical love-hate relationship existed. In 1695 a Massachusetts law required a town to be fined if it didn't have a tavern. At the same time, the first governor was publicly complaining about drunkenness in his colony.

Since then, some have constantly and loudly advocated legal alcohol sales and consumption and others, equally loudly, have objected to it. The early American frontier, however, was wide open and lonely. As unattached males migrated west, drunkenness became more common. They drank in the early days to escape boredom and loneliness, but the use became an addiction.

During the Revolutionary War alcoholism became more widespread, and afterward appeared in emerging metropolitan areas. Founded in the early 1800s, the American Temperance Society set out to fight what "demon rum" was doing to our country. The Anti-Saloon League, formed later, had a more clear purpose—to close the bars. In 1853 militant elements of these organizations formed the Prohibition party which had as its goal the elimination of the liquor industry. And finally, in 1874, one of the most successful lobbying groups in our country was formed from elements of the previous organizations. The powerful Women's Christian Temperance Union banded together to support "absolution of liquor and the triumph of Christ's Golden Rule." Primarily as a result of WCTU efforts, by 1902 every state had passed laws requiring alcohol education classes in public schools.

In the early 1900s prohibition efforts began in earnest. By 1915 it was clear that prohibition was inevitable. Five years later Congress passed the Eighteenth Amendment prohibiting the sale of alcohol. But people continued to drink and, in fact, drank more. Thirteen years later the law was declared unenforceable and prohibition was repealed.

Prohibition failed because the public and some government officials ignored it. The industry went underground and created the impetus for growth of organized crime. It also created several millionaires out of entrepreneurs who took advantage of the public's demand for alcohol. After prohibition, alcohol consumption resumed "respectable" status and drinking became more widespread and public. But the love-hate relationship continued as it does today.

> No. I don't like to smoke. I hate the smell. I just like my booze. . . . No man, I'm no druggie or nothin'. PGA is the only drug for me. . . . Yeah, pure grain alcohol.
> —David (age 15) Chapel Hill

I tend to idealize my father, even though I never knew him very well. He died when I was ten. I have discovered much more and have gotten to know him better in my adult life. I was named after him. We look alike. And according to people who knew him, we even sound alike. I have told stories about him and used him in dozens of illustrations, both in books and speaking engagements, over the years. But there is one fact I have failed to tell.

My father was an alcoholic. Some of my earliest memories are of him speaking at AA meetings in the early 1950s. Our entire family sometimes attended the meetings. At other times he and I would go alone. He was "recovering." Notice I didn't say recovered. Anyone familiar with AA philosophy knows that alcoholics never claim to be recovered. The process of recovering is considered one of perpetual growth. If someone hasn't had a drink in sixty years, he can still be an alcoholic. And at AA meetings you will often hear that idea verbalized.

"Hi. My name's John and I'm an alcoholic."

"Hi John," the crowd will respond.

"I've got thirty years of sobriety . . ." the speaker will continue.

Somehow my father got on a speaking circuit. I remember traveling all over the Southeast with him and getting to hear him begin his "story." He was an upbeat speaker and used a great deal of extemporaneous humor. His skill often came in handy because occasionally the meetings would develop into dialogues between my father and people in the audience who were drunk. My most vivid memory is of one such occasion.

We had traveled to Monroe, North Carolina, for a Sunday night meeting. It was unexpectedly warm. The small room was packed with people. Most of them were smoking, and a nicotine cloud hovered inside making the room seem warmer. I had learned to pass the time by picking out the people who I thought were drunk. There were usually several, and after the meeting my father and I compared notes.

"The guy who hadn't shaved," I would suggest.

"Yeah, he was, definitely," Dad would answer.

That night I was casing the crowd when two men entered the room accompanying a woman with her hair still in rollers and bobby pins. She wore a huge, oversized raincoat tied with a sash around the middle. As she staggered into her seat, I turned to my father sitting up front and held up one finger. He laughed and then broke eye contact to regain his composure.

He got up to speak and began quite well. He used his handkerchief to punctuate his speech, as well as to dry his forehead occasionally. After about ten minutes the inevitable happened.

"Wait just a minute," the voice interrupted my father.

I turned with the crowd in the direction of the woman's voice. She argued with the two men who had brought her in.

"Oh no," I thought to myself, "it's her." A bobby pin came loose and a strand of the woman's hair dangled in front of her eyes.

"Let her speak," my father said. "Let her ask a question."

"There," she said as she wrestled herself free from the man who attempted to subdue her. As she did, the sash came loose, opening up the raincoat. Beneath it she wore only a bra, girdle, and hosiery.

"Let me ask you this," she began.

I slumped in my chair as the audience rumbled. What's he going to do now, I thought. I looked up as my father took the handkerchief and dabbed his forehead with much more vigor than before.

The woman held her cigarette casually between the fingers of her right hand. The ashes flew as she gestured wildly. The men who had brought her in took her by the arms and began to escort her out.

"Wait!" my father shouted. "Ma'am, if you want to stay and listen, that's fine. We can talk after my speech and you can ask questions."

"See there." She pulled away from her friends and resettled in her chair.

My dad continued to swab his forehead with the handkerchief. I don't remember precisely what he said, but my mother saved the notes he used that night. The following excerpts are unedited.

"By practical application of principles laid out in these twelve steps I have managed to stay sober for today, and over 1,620 other todays. Now the fascinating thing about that is this. Since I was fifteen years old I have seldom been able to stay sober more than a few days at a time. I am an alcoholic. . . .

"The first thing I remember about drinking liquor is that I didn't particularly like the taste. But the effects the white stuff my parents had in the cabinet for Dad's rheumatism and Mother's cough made me tingle all the way to my toenails. I thought I had found peace. And in a couple of years I knew I was addicted. It was an obsession. . . .

"Alcoholism is a progressive disease of the mind, spirit, and body. The alcohol ceased to be a pleasure or luxury for me and became a necessity. I needed alcohol the way a diabetic needs insulin or someone suffering from pneumonia needs antibiotics.

"I found my drunks becoming more and more prolonged and continuously harder to shake off. Within a few years I discovered the greatest secret of all history that I was sure only a few knew. I was unfortunate enough to find the morning drink. . . . The second greatest discovery for alcoholics was the automatic transmission, for I'll never forget how my foot used to fight the clutch when I had the shakes. The problem was I couldn't afford an automatic until I got sober. . . .

"In my meager attempts to stay sober I was unhappy, miserable, and alone. Believe me, an alcoholic is the loneliest person in the world. . . . Finally on the verge of losing everyone near and dear who still cared, I called for help. And help came. . . . Then and only then did I find the true answer to my problem of drinking, the source of inner peace and the key of living one day at at time. . . . Sobriety with happiness through a program of rehabilitation of the sick alcoholic mind and soul. No more being the loneliest man in the world because there was help. . . .

"A program for living, and loving and laughing again. Seeking serenity and peace. It is a way of life—the way of life for me, an alcoholic."

> We used to sneak it out of the cabinet and drink it in my room. That's really how I started. I'd drink till I passed out or got sick. That was when I was just a kid.
>
> — Patricia (age 14) Orlando

How Widespread Is the Problem of Alcohol Abuse Today?

Approximately 100 million Americans are regular consumers of alcohol. Beyond doubt, it is the number one psychoactive, mind-altering drug in this country. For thousands of years it has been the traditional high of Western culture. Social consumption of alcohol is thoroughly integrated into the substance of life itself. In many areas the local bar or "pub" remains the center for socializing. Alcohol is associated with many ceremonies and rituals of American life. Weddings, holidays, and religious rites all use alcohol as elements of celebration. It is not this use of alcohol, however, that leads to problems.

Alcohol is a colorless liquid found in beer, wine, and liquor. The beverage form is a compound of grain alcohol. Most people consider alcohol a stimulant, but actually it's a highly addictive depressant. It acts by reducing activity in the central nervous system and is very similar to its chemical cousin ether, an anesthetic used in medicine to induce unconsciousness. In fact, ether is made from alcohol. When you drink alcohol you are basically drinking an anesthetic.

> I eat onion rings and mints, so they can't smell it on my breath. . . . I don't know, I just like to get drunk. My parents don't like it, but you know, all my friends drink.
> — Dana (age 17) Nashville

The effects of alcohol vary with its percentage in the blood. The legal measure of drunkenness is 1/10th of 1 percent alcohol concentrated in the bloodstream. The amount of alcohol needed to cause this concentration varies with a person's size. A 150-pound man would normally require 4 beers, 4 glasses of wine, or 4 ounces of liquor to register .10. By the time a person is intoxicated at this level, two effects have occurred. First, inhibitions have disappeared, allowing certain behaviors to surface. Some people become amorous, some boisterous, and others belligerent. Second, judgment and the ability to think abstractly have disappeared.

If the blood alcohol level continues to climb, the depressant effects become more obvious. People begin to stumble as they lose coordination and muscle control. Bodily responses slow down significantly. Speech becomes slurred. Judgment becomes further impaired, and emotional control is lost. Guilt, fear, and remorse lose their psychic power, freeing people of all feelings of anxiety. This pleasant freedom is probably one element in the addictive power of alcohol. If alcohol consumption continues, psychomotor coordination decreases. Dizziness, loss of muscle control, and unconsciousness follow. Were consumption to continue beyond this point, death would occur.

Approximately fifteen million Americans are addicted to alcohol, according to the Drug Enforcement Administration and the National Institute of Alcohol Abuse and Alcoholism. The same organizations state that there are an additional 4.6 million problem drinkers in our country. Over 100,000 people die each year from the effects of alcohol. An alcoholic has a life expectancy 10–22 years shorter than a non-drinker. Up to 83 percent of all fire-related deaths are considered to be alcohol related, and 50 percent of all home accidents are caused by problem drinkers. Alcohol is a factor in 70 percent of all drownings and 40 percent of all industrial accidents. Over 15,000 adult suicides and 3,000 teenage suicides are committed each year by alcoholics. And NIDA estimates there are four million problem drinkers among teenagers.

I worked in a drug treatment center in Southern California for approximately three years. During that period, through family groups, patient groups, and individual counseling I worked with over a hundred adolescents. Some cases had happy endings, others did not. A few were true horror stories. But none seem as incomplete as my experience with Rachel.

She was fourteen the first time we met and had been

admitted by her parents for drug-abuse treatment. Described as
a binge drinker, Rachel remained sober most of the time.
However, every month or so she would drink continuously for
two to three days. Prior to her first admission she had
consumed a quart of whiskey, a gallon of wine, and two six-
packs of beer every day for a week. She had suffered memory
loss, "shakes," and hallucinations as she tried unsuccessfully
to dry herself out from the binge. In fear, Rachel's parents
hospitalized her for detoxification.

Rachel was fourteen going on thirty. Her eyes sank deeply
above her hollow cheeks. Her hair was ragged and matted.
When conscious she spoke like a trooper who had fought one
too many battles.

"Time to go," she moaned. "I'm awake, right? This must be
detox. I'm going to live. Who brought me in?"

"Your parents," I answered.

"And who are you supposed to be," she said more as a
statement than a question.

"I'm supposed to be John, but it really doesn't matter," I
responded. "You need some rest."

"Gotta go," she mumbled returning to sleep. I shook my
head and left.

The next day, I discovered Rachel's parents had taken her
home. Concerned, I began asking questions. Another counselor
explained that Rachel had been in detox on two other
occasions, beginning when she was eleven. Before I left, two
years later, she was admitted three other times. On each
admission I discussed a treatment program with her parents.
They adamantly refused help. Two or three days to detoxify
and Rachel was taken home.

I enjoyed the few conversations I had with this spunky
child. Rachel was bright enough to know she needed help, but
still her parents refused. There was nothing the staff could do.
After I moved we lost contact. Two years later a former
colleague updated me. Rachel was still alive, but her addiction
was worsening. She had been suffering blackouts, was staying
drunk longer, had wrecked three cars, and had been arrested

for public intoxication. She had last been admitted several months earlier when brought in by an ambulance after passing out in a downtown alley. She left the hospital three days later and had not been heard from since.

While writing this book I called again. Nobody had seen Rachel since that time. One person thought she had been injured in an accident. Someone else said the entire family had moved out of the area. Another thought Rachel had entered college. Whatever the case, she was gone. The family phone had been disconnected. It was all incomplete. I could detach myself emotionally and say after all, "Rachel is one of fifteen million Americans who is an alcoholic." By making her a statistic, perhaps the pain would be less. But like all the others in this book and in the figures I mention, Rachel is a person. She's flesh and blood. She has a personality. She is real. And again, there's nothing I can do. It haunts me.

What Types of Teenagers Are Most Likely to Abuse Alcohol?

Alcohol is the drug teens are most likely to abuse. As hard drugs receive more notoriety, anxious parents see drinking as a safer alternative. Many adults not only tolerate, but sanction alcohol use among children. The atmosphere has led to a sharp increase in adolescent and even early childhood drinking. According to the Second Report of the National Commission on Marijuana and Drug Abuse, over 90 percent of high school seniors have experimented with alcohol at least once. Most adolescent drinking occurs on special occasions until the tenth grade. After that, teenagers prefer to drink at parties and with friends. Much teenage drinking occurs in homes when parents are out for an evening or away for a weekend.

One study conducted several years ago among students found two major groups likely to become problem drinkers. In today's adolescent vernacular they would be referred to as "preppies" and "hoods." Those labeled preppies are oriented toward social aspects of school life and non-athletic, unsuper-

vised extracurricular activities. Those labeled hoods are teenagers oriented toward social activities not sanctioned by the
school, who often skip classes, and who disrupt class when
they *do* attend.

The study suggested that both groups were more likely to
become involved in problem drinking than those students
who: (1) seldom attended unsupervised parties; (2) belonged
to a clique involved in performing arts or cultural activity;
(3) were immersed in competition for good grades;
(4) participated in extracurricular activities requiring verbal
skills, such as newspaper or yearbook; (5) dated regularly;
(6) were involved in competitive sports. The researchers
found that the preppie and hood groups accounted for about
90 percent of regular juvenile alcohol consumption.

Although this particular study did not suggest the reasons
for the abusive drinking of these two groups, its implications
are important. Both groups participated primarily in peer
activity that did not involve adult relationships. Likewise,
neither group was involved in self-esteem building activities.
The lack of opportunity for significant adult relationships may
be the most important factor. These relationships were absent
in the lives of both the "preppies" and "hoods."

> *I go out drinking most of the time. Last week
> we had a keg party at a friend's house. I didn't
> know a lot of people there. There was about
> thirty or so, but I get off on meeting people
> anyway. It was a good way to meet girls and
> pass time.*
>
> *— Bert (age 16) Evansville*

"It's difficult, John," he began, "to admit you're powerless
over something. Can you imagine what it does to your self-
concept? To admit you've been whipped by—well, really, by
yourself? Much less a bottle. Of course it was me who picked it
up. I was the one who did that."

Frank picked up his fork and played with the lima beans on

his plate. "Have you ever noticed how tasteless limas are?" he laughed.

"Yes, I've noticed that. So you started when you were little, right?"

"Right," he responded. "I started drinking with my dad. He thought it was cool, I guess, to feed a three year old beer. I started drinking then and really never stopped. After I started to school they didn't think it was so cute. But hey, I was hooked by then! It never really slowed me down. I snuck drinks even in the first grade all the way through high school— army—college—the whole works. Would you believe by the time I was twenty-eight I had been drinking for twenty-five years? Most people think that's drunk talk."

"No," I answered him. "I believe it. Probably a year ago I wouldn't have, but I do now. You want my limas?" I teased.

We laughed as he placed one on the edge of his spoon and flipped it across the table at me. "Watch out," he teased. "I'm deadly from thirty paces."

"I've been wondering about something," I began. "You had a lot going for you as a kid. You were an athlete, you had a scholarship. Your parents were well off. Why did you keep on drinking? What was it? I mean, were you drinking to drink, or drinking to get away from something, or what?"

"Aw, John," he responded. "You know that probably better than I do. You knew me when I was a drunk. Why don't you tell me?"

I stared at him for a moment. "No," I smiled. "You're not going to hook me on that one. I'm interviewing you, remember? Come on Frank, what was it?"

"Well," he responded. "We both know I had crap for self-esteem. I really never did a thing on my own. I made grades because Dad paid for a tutor. I was an athlete because I was lucky enough to go to a private school that pumped me up. That was as much because of my last name as anything else. All my life I was compared to my father. I got his name, his looks, and inherited his business.

"Drinking was a habit, but it was a habit that allowed me to get away. I guess it was a great stress reliever. I hated myself even in elementary school. I couldn't stand the way I looked and acted and was treated. Really, I think, I wanted to be normal. My dad drank, and I hated him. But the more I hated him, the more I became like him.

"So, I drank because I couldn't stand myself or my dad. And I drank to relieve the pain. And I drank to drink. I was really hooked bad, John. You know that."

I thought back ten years. "Yeah, I remember. Does it bother you to talk about it?"

"No. As long as I think it will help somebody. I don't like drunk talk. You know, like telling war stories."

"Me either," I assured him. "So what would you say to parents to help them if their kid is drinking or to help them prevent their kid from drinking?"

Frank thought before answering. He took his fork and pierced several lima beans.

"It's like these limas," he began. "I don't care for them. But that's me. You see, they're okay. They're just fine the way they are. My personal taste is irrelevant. It's them, the limas, that are important. You take one of these buggers and accept it and love it and care for it because it's just fine.

"And you don't compare it to other limas, or pintos, or green beans, or potatoes. It's special and perfect just like it is. It doesn't have to conform to my expectations to be okay. It doesn't have to look like the other limas, or taste like cornbread, or anything. And for God's sake, don't try to make coleslaw out of a lima. It just won't work. If you do that to your lima, you ruin it and the coleslaw. The lima has its own purpose, its own identity, its own meaning. So don't mess with it."

Frank looked at the ceiling for a moment and then back down at me. "I think if my parents had known that, I wouldn't have needed to drink. And I think if I'd been treated like that I would not have chosen to continue drinking.

"So that's what I would say to other parents. I'm forty years old and I wasted most of my life. Take it from a lima bean who's been there." Frank stuck the limas into his mouth, reached for the cassette recorder between us, and turned it off.

> *It goes like this—social drinking; nightly drinking; drinking to feel good; sneaking drinks; drinking to feel normal; breakfast drinking; constant drinking. It's a dad-burn whirlwind, that's what it is.*
> —*Joe (age 22) Mobile*

What Is an Alcoholic?

Not everyone who drinks becomes addicted. Alcoholics are people who lose control or can't control their drinking behavior. Some experts say this is determined by a genetic predisposition. Others refer to it as a disease and compare it to diabetes. The diabetic has an adverse reaction to sugar and has to control his intake. Most diabetics have to abstain from sugar. Similarly, alcoholics have an adverse reaction to alcohol and must abstain from drinking it. An alcoholic literally lets the drinking control him or her.

The term "problem drinker" is equally imprecise. Used primarily to describe anyone whose drinking causes problems, it leaves out those who can control their drinking, even though drinking may have caused them difficulty in the past or is likely to in the future. Problems can occur regardless of the amount of alcohol consumed. Most experts agree that a person can develop alcoholism or be born with the malady. Either way, if addiction (or alcoholism) occurs, total abstinence is the only solution. Alcoholics cannot participate in "social drinking."

Each of the fifteen million alcoholics in this country affects at least four other people, usually family members or colleagues. Approximately two of three alcoholics are male, but the number of females is increasing rapidly. Regardless of stereotypes or publicity, only five percent of those affected by alcoholism are skid row bums. Most are relatively ordinary people and, in fact, one out of ten social drinkers is an alcoholic.

What Are the Symptoms of Alcohol Addiction?

A person who demonstrates any degree of distress or anxiety when he or she is unable to continue drinking is likely addicted. Combined with an increased tolerance, this usually signals serious addiction. If a person is addicted, abstaining from alcohol can produce severe physiological pains, including rapid heartbeat, nausea, and possible muscle spasms. These withdrawal symptoms can develop into a serious condition called delirium tremens (DT's). There is no real understanding as to how alcohol causes this condition, which is often accompanied by hallucinations and tremors. In addition to the risk of withdrawal, alcohol can damage the liver, brain cells, and other body tissue. In fact, one out of five adult deaths today is caused by cirrhosis of the liver, a disease attributed almost solely to alcoholism.

Alcoholism exacts its highest cost from the family of the drinker. The emotional treadmill of pain, guilt, and disappointment never stops to allow the family of the alcoholic to rest and gain strength. As a parent, an alcoholic is inconsistent and unpredictable, leaving the children confused and anxious. As these children become adults they often have tremendous difficulty with their own emotions and relationships. Often these symptoms appear identical to those of alcoholism, even in the absence of drinking. Wives, husbands, parents, and children of alcoholics all have above average levels of physical and emotional illness. Alcoholic families experience a higher frequency of separation, divorce, and family violence. According to the Department of Health Education and Welfare, 52 percent of violent husbands had histories of problem drinking or alcoholism and over 65 percent of child-abuse cases are alcohol related.

There is no such thing as the "typical" alcoholic. Alcoholics range in age from as young as six years old to senior citizens.

Alcoholism is non-discriminating and can affect anyone. Statistics, however, do indicate certain trends.

Most alcoholics are male. Half have attended college. Most women who develop alcoholism associate their drinking with situational stress such as divorce, death of a friend, or job difficulty. Women are also more likely to drink alone than are their male counterparts. The largest portion of alcoholics and problem drinkers fall in the 35–50 age bracket. The second largest grouping is teens. There is more drinking in urban areas than in small towns, and there is more in small towns than in rural areas.

Geographically, the highest proportion of drinkers lives in the Northeast and Mid-Atlantic states. The West and Midwest have intermediate rates of alcohol consumption. The lowest rate of drinking is in the South. More alcohol is consumed in middle and upper levels of the socioeconomic strata. However, more problem drinking is reported in the lower strata.

A similar comparison is found in religious groups. A comparatively larger amount of alcohol is consumed by those claiming to be Jewish, Lutheran, and Episcopalian. Yet, generally speaking, these groups have lower rates of problem drinkers or alcoholics.

Fundamentalist Protestant groups have a lower level of alcohol consumption but a higher proportion of problem drinkers. As an example, Baptists and Mormons are less likely than the general population to drink. But once they begin drinking they are more likely to become problem drinkers.

This data leads to no concrete solutions. There is no universally accepted scientific theory to explain why one person can drink periodically for years and have no difficulty and another becomes addicted immediately. Just as there are many different kinds of alcoholics, there are many different theories of alcoholism. The only common trait all alcoholics share is their obsession for beverage alcohol and a compulsive drinking pattern.

*I got really drunk one night in Birmingham.
Three days later I found myself in Dallas. I had
no idea how I got there. I still, to this day,
don't know. That's when I thought I might
have a problem.*

— Beth (age 23) Fort Wayne

What Are the Stages of Alcohol Addiction?

In 1946, E. M. Jellinek completed a classical study on the
progression of alcoholism. He interviewed over 2,000 alcoholics during his research. As yet, no one has improved the
model of drinking he developed years ago.

Jellinech described the first phase as periodic drinking.
Some 90 percent of all alcoholics began by social drinking.
This may be occasionally excessive, yet remain social in
nature. The second phase involves memory and concentration
problems and possible "blackouts." Blackouts are when problem drinkers remain conscious and ambulatory but have no
memory of what they do. About the time blackouts start,
alcoholics may begin sneaking drinks in an attempt to hide the
actual amount of alcohol consumption.

At this point most drinkers begin to worry about what others
think of their drinking. This concern begins a campaign of
rationalizing, denying, or blaming something or someone other
than themselves. This is accompanied or closely followed by a
change in the pattern or style of drinking—from beer to wine,
from evening to weekends, from home to bar—as the alcoholic
rationalizes that a change will solve the problem. The gimmick
fails, but rationalization continues as the alcoholic decides
morning drinks will get him or her going. This results in binge
drinking. Defeat follows this phase. The alcoholic's life centers
on drinking. Delirium tremens, liver disease, brain damage,
and death follow.

Or the alcoholic begins to recover.

My counseling relationship with Walter continued for several months. Eventually he did face court proceedings. He was placed on probation and required to complete a long-term drug treatment program and to perform over 100 hours of community service. The treatment program chosen by the judge was an out-of-state, inpatient facility. Walter left immediately to begin rehabilitation, and I figured that would be the last I would hear from him.

Four months later I was surprised by his telephone call. "John Baucom," he growled, "this is Walter Smith. How in the world are you?"

"Walter!" I exclaimed. "I never expected to hear from you. What's been happening? How was treatment?" I knew the facility he'd been sent to had a reputation for being about as gentle as Marine Corps boot camp.

"Man," he moaned, "it was absolutely awful and beautiful at the same time. You know, it's one of those things I'm glad I went through, and wouldn't trade for a million bucks, but at the same time I'd hate for a friend to have to go through it. You know?"

"Yeah, I've had some experiences like that myself." I paused while my mind wandered back to the jungles of Vietnam—

"You still there?" Walter interrupted.

"Sorry about that," I apologized. "So what are you up to? Are you handling everything okay? What's different in your life now?" I wanted to ask if he was staying straight, but decided to wait.

"Everything's different, big guy. I'm not crazy anymore mainly. Insanity doesn't have a hold on me. Got a lot of family stuff to work on, but I'll take it one day at a time. It's a long way back, John," he sighed. "Got to change everything. Friends, school, job. They all gotta go. But it's all worth it. I finally got what I was looking for all these years. That's the main thing I learned in treatment."

I wondered if I had missed something he had said. "What was it, Walter? What were you looking for in that trash dumpster?"

"Peace of mind, John, and it ain't in no drug."

Questions for Inquiry

1. How have your previous assumptions concerning the alcohol problem in our country changed since reading this chapter?
2. What financial, emotional, or physiological costs have your family experienced related to alcohol?
3. How many of your friends would you consider to be problem drinkers? How do you support their problem? What have you done to help them face their problem?
4. What is your personal awareness of the alcohol problem in your community? Do you know how local industries and businesses support or help alcoholics and problem drinkers? What services are available, locally, to help problem drinkers and their families (i.e., AA/Alanon/Alateen)?
5. Who in your community is making money from alcohol or other drugs? In what ways do you protest or accept this?

Family or Group Activity

Contact a local Alcoholics Anonymous or Alanon group and find out where and when an "open" meeting will be held. Attend the meeting as a family, including all adolescent and school-age children. Use the following questions as a basis for a family discussion: How did you feel about attending the meeting? How did it affect your perception of what an alcoholic or drug addict is? Why do you think AA has been so successful? How did the meeting affect your opinion of yourself? Of what compulsive behavior in your own life did it make you aware?

Journal Entry

Calculate how much money you spent on drugs (including over-the-counter medications, alcohol, cigarettes, and caffeine) in the last week or month. Consider other ways to spend this money. Post on your refrigerator either a picture of the object you would like to buy or a description of how you plan to use the money you could save by not using the substances mentioned above. Study the picture or description at least twice a day and say to yourself: "This _____ is the goal for my drug money this week." Keep a daily record in your journal of how successful you are in sticking to your goal.

Comment again on your experience of going "drug free" while reading this book.

For Further Thought

In our fast-paced, sophisticated world, we tend not to become emotionally involved in a cause unless we are personally affected. As a person already concerned about the drug problem, how can you influence friends, neighbors, and family members to watch more closely for signs of adolescent needs and to listen more carefully for subtle cries for help?

Drunkenness is temporary suicide; the happiness that it brings is merely negative, a momentary cessation of unhappiness.
— *Bertrand Russell,* The Conquest of Happiness

4

YOUR CHILD AND DRUG ABUSE

- Why do children use drugs?
- What is addiction?
- What is dependence?
- Are my children in a high- or low-risk category?

"Listen you guys," I said to the noisy group. "I want you to just talk for a few minutes about how you learned to begin using drugs. And I want you to think about your answers. This is important and we're here to help other folks. Who knows? Maybe what you say will save somebody's life. So believe it, this is very serial."

Several of the teenagers laughed and punched each other. "Hey, be serial!" Paul joked.

"Okay," I resumed. "Paul, why don't you start and the rest of you just chime in. What do you think about it, buddy? What were the major influences in your life that helped you along? How did you learn to deal with life by using drugs?"

"I don't know," he responded. "A lot of my buddies did reefer and at the time I was with them a lot. They fired one up and started passing it around. I just couldn't say no. I was the last one and everybody else had taken a hit off it. So the pressure was on me. So I did it to be cool."

"That's pretty much true for me too," Tim added. "The first time I did anything was at home. I snuck a drink or two from the liquor cabinet. All my buddies were doing it, so I did too. It was like initiation into the club that you had to drink till you passed out. I wanted to do it to be 'in.' I couldn't pass out though. I just kept on and on and pretty soon I kind of went crazy. I never passed out or anything, but I scared the bejees out of the other dudes who were with me."

"Tim, how old were you then?" I asked.

"I was, let's see, when that happened I was nine," he responded.

"And you're seventeen now, right?" I asked. "And how about the rest of you, sixteen and seventeen? Is there anybody here younger than sixteen? So far it sounds like friends were the big influence, and of course with you, Tim, it was your parents too, right?"

"Definitely," he answered. "And we're all working on it now. Sort of like a family project, I guess."

"For me it was different," Tanya began. "I wanted to model. I had the height, but I was heavy. Well, I thought I was heavy anyway. Nobody else did. But I kept looking at the models on TV and in the magazines—Seventeen, Self, and Cosmo. Compared to them I looked heavy. So I started using diet pills and then went on to cocaine because it was supposed to make you speed and I thought I could lose more weight that way. I know that was sick and all that. I'm over it now. But that's how sick I was. And I was really by myself. So I didn't have much of any friend's influence."

"Jackie, how about you? How does your situation compare with these?"

"Well, I guess I was somewhere in between," he suggested. "Where I grew up everybody was on drugs. In Newport that's just the way it is. You can ask anybody who's been there, it's just something you fall into. I don't think I ever even knew anybody who was straight until I was in school. I guess middle school or something."

"Did you ever look for straight people?" I questioned. "Did you ever think about looking for a way out?"

"No," he responded quickly. "It's not like that. I mean it never crosses your mind. I never knew anything else was there. . . ."

"Couldn't you have gone to church or something?" Tanya asked. "You make it sound like nothing was your fault, Jackie. That's denying responsibility. You had a choice. Nobody made you keep on like that."

"I know that," Jackie responded. "But Dr. B wants to know how we learned and that's how I learned. Besides, when I knew I could choose, I did. Look where I am now."

"Okay," I interrupted. "Jackie, how about it? Didn't you know anybody who went to church or anything like that? You must have known someone who wasn't doing drugs. I know it's bad, but not everybody is high."

"Ask Christie," he said, gesturing. "She's been there. Is it like that or what?" The tension heightened as we all turned toward Christie.

> Just say no? It ain't that easy, man.
> — Kira (age 17) Bismarck

Why Do Children Use Drugs?

Most childhood and adolescent drinking begins quite innocently. In one study of over 7,000 senior high school students, curiosity was found to be the primary culprit for both drinking and drug use. Whether or not drug use continues, however, depends on several factors, primarily friends and family. If peers and parents drink or use drugs the adolescent is likely to continue.

By adolescence, peer influence may be more significant than parental use. Yet, the highest rates of abuse were registered among teens whose parents and friends alike used alcohol or other drugs.

A University of Southern California study found peer drug use to be highly important both in introducing children to drugs as well as reinforcing continued use. A study of 8,000 high school students in the state of New York found similar results. Of those students who reported no close friends using marijuana, less than 2 percent themselves used drugs. Seventeen percent of those who said they had a "few" friends who used drugs, were themselves users. Fifty percent of those who reported "some" of their friends as users had used drugs themselves.

The percentage of drug users continued to rise with the number of reported friends who were drug oriented. Eighty percent of the individuals questioned reported drug use if most of their friends were drug oriented. Finally, if they reported "all" of their friends as drug oriented, over 90 percent admitted using drugs themselves. This study also found the number of weekly visits with drug-oriented friends also had an impact on youth drug use. Dozens of other studies have found identical results.

> *Everybody else seemed so happy. Friends and TV stuff. I was down, way low, and everybody else was great. It was Christmas, so I said, "Hey, why not?" And so I started getting high.*
> *— Martie (age 13) Madison*

Most teens who become chronic abusers experience a high degree of boredom, alienation, and anger. At the same time they lack imagination, energy, and creativity. With other drug-using friends, these children find both an escape from their pain and acceptance from their peer group. The continued use of drugs masks the depression, stress, and lack of confidence these youngsters often experience. In this way the drug becomes seductively addicting both socially and physiologically. But it seldom begins that way.

One expert in the drug treatment field described adolescent and young adult drug abusers as "basically immature, dependent kinds of people. Very impulsive, low in self-control—the kind of people who want what they want when they want it. These are very angry people who give you the idea they were spoiled as children and never outgrew it, actually." During the same discussion another authority described childhood drug abusers as "youngsters whose need for emotional security is just not met very well. There's not enough love, not enough reinforcement, and not enough good stable security. I think these babies are just scared to death and drugs are a way out."

> *You got to have something to make it. Everything is moving too fast. That's why I started doing speed. To keep up with everything. You know, to cope, to make it.*
> *—Billy (age 14) Germantown*

"Here we are," my guide said. "This is the Green Room, and this is your dressing room."

I glanced at the door. DR. JOHN BAUCOM, it read. "Wow," I said aloud. "That's nice."

"You'll need make-up. Someone will get you in a few minutes. There's fruit and finger food in the Green Room. Make yourself comfortable."

As I turned to find the fruit, an attractive woman pulled my elbow. "Are you Dr. Baucom?" she asked. Without awaiting my answer she continued to speak. "I'll be taking care of your make-up. Everyone else is already finished. Come on with me."

I followed obediently, more out of fear of getting lost in the labyrinth of hallways I'd just come through than anything else. I had been on television before, but never on a popular nationally syndicated program like *Hour Magazine*. I was learning, however, that they all had one repulsive detail in common: make-up.

"You know," I began, bargaining, "I've got a pretty good tan. You really think I need this?"

"Look," she said, "I've done make-up for John Madden, Mike Ditka, and The Fridge." She stared, almost defiantly.

I glanced down at her and smiled. "You got me," I surrendered. "If it's good enough for John Madden, it's good enough for me."

We both laughed as we entered the make-up room.

"You're talking about teenagers today, right?" she asked.

"Uh-huh."

"I've got two myself," she said as she worked. "You know about drug abuse?"

"A little," I admitted. "I've worked in that area for quite a few years. But there's so much to know. It's difficult to be an expert."

"The dimple in your chin is going to look dark on the screen," she complained. "Let me fix that." She searched through her tray for "dimple fixer" and then continued to work her magic. "What's the best thing I can do to help my kids stay off drugs? I think they're straight. My husband and I don't drink or anything. They make good grades. They're really no problem. But there's so much of that now. I know a lot of their friends do drugs. They even get some from their own parents. You have no idea what it's like out here."

"I know it's bad," I agreed. "I went to school here. It really sounds like you're doing a lot of things right. I guess if I could give teenagers something to help it would be three things—a high degree of self-confidence, a sense of competence, and probably persistence. If kids have those qualities I think they have less need to seek dependence or strength in some drug. Independence is what we want. Not drug-dependent children."

"That's beautiful!" she exclaimed. "Are you going to be talking about that on the show?"

"No." I shook my head. "I don't think so."

"Well, you should. You'll have to do that the next trip."

"Next trip?" I asked. We both laughed.

"Dr. Baucom?" a voice called out. "You ready to go? You're on."

I sighed and took a deep breath.

> It started when my boyfriend and I would have problems and like I'd worry and stuff. And I knew Mom would always have some kind of downer in her bathroom. I didn't know what they were all the time. But, you know, Valium, Nembutal, Seconal, Miltown. Before long, I'm gone.
>
> — Lynn (age 17) Jackson

What Is Addiction?

Addiction is a biochemical and physiological process by which a person can develop a cellular "oneness" with a foreign chemical. The substance actually joins with a person's body to the point that to "feel normal" new supplies of the substance must be consumed. If not replenished, the addict experiences physiological withdrawal symptoms. In many ways the reaction can be as dramatic as if part of the addict's anatomy was amputated. These reactions may also include emotional pain, but are not limited to emotions. Withdrawal can cause a variety of visceral responses, including shaking, chills, sweating, seizures, convulsions, increased heart rate, craving for the drug, and possibly even death. Addiction is deadly and, in fact, the Latin root word "addictus" means slave.

> I just didn't think I was addicted. They were prescription drugs. My husband was a doctor. You don't think about it with prescription drugs, even if you do get them from your husband. Addicted people are drunks and junkies. I wasn't like that.
>
> — Lana (age 28) Destin

Anyone can learn to become a drug addict. No discrimination is made for race, age, gender, or socioeconomic level. Wealthy and advantaged matriarchs to skid row bums and all assortments in between are represented by the alcoholic/drug addict label. On the surface these addicted people may appear quite different. But beyond superficial levels, surprising similarities exist.

Drug-addicted people live perpetually "on the edge." They are forced to constantly manipulate, "con," and lie merely to survive. Much of their time is spent in either overtly illegal or at least questionable activity. Their behavior and habits need to be disguised a majority of the time. Deception becomes a way of life. The chronic addict or alcoholic gets a great deal of practice and ultimately becomes extremely effective at lying. In fact, they can even develop a charming and entertaining side to their misrepresentations. Obviously, they have to fool their families, police, teachers, supervisors, each other, and the rest of society. As a result, they become skilled at it.

What Is Dependence?

Whereas addiction is a biochemical process, dependence is more psychological and social. It can occur with people, objects, or substances and in many ways is more dangerous than addiction due to the lack of physical symptoms as evidence of the problem. Addiction can occur with tobacco, alcohol, or any other drug. Dependence can occur with music, food, drugs, or relationships. Most authorities in the field believe that people who become addicted (or problem users) of drugs have unmet dependency needs. For whatever reasons, dependent people lack confidence to face the challenges of life and therefore use some chemical for assistance. The addict's crutch does not necessarily begin as a drug. It can begin as a person. It can even begin as a parent. That was how it happened with Irene, the mother of Holly, whose story I told in chapter 1.

Irene was the youngest of five children and the only

daughter of a very protective father. "I was the center of my father's life," Irene once told me. "I got everything I wanted and a lot more. It was a mutual admiration society."

Her father went beyond loving Irene. He idolized her to the point of not allowing her to do much of anything for herself. He constantly praised her in glittering generalities. Yet being called "the most precious girl in the world" and "Daddy's little girl" did little for Irene's self-esteem. Even as a youngster she recognized his praise as meaningless and untrue. Since she was never allowed to face life's challenges alone, Irene had no sense of personal competency. She saw herself as inadequate. Receiving without question from her father everything she asked for made Irene impulsive and impatient. If something went wrong at school or in personal relationships, her father ran interference and blamed others involved. As a result, her friendships suffered. And since Irene had no opportunity to make decisions on her own, she also suffered from a poor sense of judgment.

At the age of nineteen, Irene married her first boyfriend. He was thirty and even more domineering than her father. He abused her mercilessly and wouldn't let her out of his control. They moved to a secluded rural area and he left her daily without transportation. She was continually accused of being unfaithful and of other imagined wrongs. When Irene became pregnant, her husband beat her less, but after their daughter's birth the beatings resumed and rapidly worsened.

Irene had become so dependent that leaving or ending the marriage was out of the question. In her mind, being on her own was not even an option. Her father, who had opposed her marriage, turned his back on Irene after she disobeyed him. So she turned to her husband for approval. He responded with fear and anger. She could count on his cycle of regular weekend drunks and subsequent beatings.

When Irene eventually met Jan, her nearest neighbor, she learned that Jan's life was a mirror image of her own. She too had married an older man. In fact, he was friends with Irene's husband. Jan and Irene easily gained each other's friendship.

Jan had a car and began secretly taking Irene into town almost daily. They stopped by Jan's parents where Irene met Bobby, Jan's recently divorced older brother. He and Irene became close friends. One morning Irene was visibly upset after a fight with her husband. Bobby offered her several Valium. Irene described her first Valium trip as if it had been a religious experience.

"It was gorgeous," she exclaimed. "I never felt anything so good. I thought I had died and gone to heaven. For the first time in two years I was able to relax and for the first time in my life I liked myself. I could depend on Valium."

Irene also thought she could depend on Bobby. Their relationship grew and became more important to her. Soon she was pregnant again, this time with Bobby's child. Her drug use progressed, and within a month she left her husband and moved in with Bobby. He became her drug supplier and lover. He introduced her to the needle, and heroin became her new drug of choice.

The baby was stillborn, but the tragedy had almost no impact on Irene's life. As her dependency and addiction increased, the demands she made on Bobby mushroomed. Soon he was physically abusing her. To medicate herself, Irene increased her level of drug use. The cycle intensified and finally, after leaving Bobby, she moved to a city in the Northeast, where heroin was said to be more plentiful. Eventually, through a new boyfriend, she found a well-paying assembly line job. Within three months she was injured and placed on worker's compensation. Her employer never discovered that the accident was caused by her drug-slowed reactions.

Before entering a treatment program, Irene had no idea she had any problem other than drug addiction. Certainly the heroin and polydrug addictions were problems, but Irene's problems were far more complex. She was dependent. The object of her dependence was irrelevant. Whether it was a man, a drug, or worker's compensation did not matter. If her dependency needs were not addressed she would never overcome heroin or any other biochemical addiction. Anyone can go through detoxification. But another fix is only a dependent decision away.

Like other addicts, dependent people have an unconscious wish to be protected. They want to be nourished and taken care of. They have difficulty making individual decisions and are inclined to lean on others for advice, guidance, and support. At times a severely dependent person appears to want to be absorbed or united with a stronger person. As many philosophers have suggested, we are "at our finest" when involved in a meaningful relationship. But there is a major difference between this healthy type of relationship and one based on dependency needs.

Irene is only one example of dependent people who become addicted to drugs or enter destructive relationships. It is one of the most common and most frequent behavioral patterns I see in counseling. As a result, I have come to believe that the most positive way to help young people is to guide them toward independence.

> *Really you have to be pretty strong to say no. Say there's some boy you like and you finally get a date with him and he wants you to drink. I mean you don't want him to think you're weird or something. He might not ask you out again, you know?*
> —Jane (age 15) Glendale

Are My Children in a High- or Low-risk Category?

Independence is not a bad word. It does not mean stubborn or uncontrollable. In this book it refers to a child who can make decisions without being adversely influenced by peers; does not find it necessary to lean on other people for advice or to feel complete; and does not rely on drugs or alcohol to survive. Independent people have no interest in drugs. They have no reason to risk personal health and autonomy. Those who feel such a degree of competence are not candidates for drug abuse.

Independent, healthy adolescents have various characteristics in common. These traits have been chosen by surveys of people in the teaching and helping professions, as well as by looking statistically at personality traits of children who are addicted. By closely viewing this pool of teenagers, we can more clearly understand what does and does not lead to healthy independence.

(1) Independent children view themselves as worthwhile. All the other characteristics are built upon this foundation. When children are growing toward independence, their self-esteem is constantly increasing. They believe without hesitation that they "count." This has to do with their internal belief of self-worth. It is not something parents can give, but they can help.

Research studies have illustrated time and again that drug-abusing children have low self-esteem. They don't like themselves and don't believe anyone else does either. They report themselves as bored and fail to find enthusiasm in any area of life. In fact, this characteristic is so significant that the only drug-prevention programs to experience any success are those promoting self-worth and autonomy.

Parents can believe their children are worthwhile and special. They can hold their children in high regard. Yet, unless the children themselves "feel" the worth internally, it doesn't exist for them. The mistakes I have seen most American parents make in this area lie in two extremes. We're either overly involved to the point of meddling or woefully uninvolved. A healthy balance is possible, although it rarely exists.

Overinvolved parents tell their children exactly what to do, how to do it, and when it needs to be done. This tendency to over-instruct and follow too closely fails to allow time and space for children to solve problems by experimentation. We make life too easy by solving their problems for them. Children raised in this environment learn to believe that it is unnecessary to attempt personal problem solving because "someone will come to the rescue." Such children are handicapped in a society that requires young adults to function independently.

At the other extreme, American parents often are uninvolved in mentoring their children. We fail to lead them through levels of problem-solving skills, leaving them to fend for themselves with inadequate preparation. Through much painful trial and error and with persistence they may come to believe the world is frightening because no one is there to help. No one pays attention to their struggles. Such children, if left to struggle through developmental years, will be ill-equipped to form satisfying relationships, to interact with others, and consequently to cooperate with others to solve problems.

Parents would do best to consider their children as apprentices of life. This requires that we involve ourselves in their activity to instruct and guide as needed. Then we must stand back and allow them to apply their learning. We may step in prior to the point of their frustration, but it is important that we not step in before they have exhausted their curiosity.

(2) Independent children have a sense of identity within a social network. They are sure of their role in the family and in the community. They are surrounded by a strong network of family, extended kin, and friends, but not "owned" by a family or home. The family is around them emotionally for support and love. The relationships are close, but not symbiotic. Independent children know they are a part of the larger world, but also that they are different. They find it unnecessary to resort to radical appearance or behavior to establish separateness or identity. Parents can clarify for their children from an early age their place in the family and the world by giving them a safe family environment in which to function.

Parents may also need to provide an artificial extended family. Research has shown that the most healthy children are those who have several significant adult relationships in which they feel safe. Most Americans today do not live in an extended family network where these relationships automatically exist. Societies that still have this arrangement have less frequent and less serious problems with adolescent stress. Parents can compensate for a missing extended family by inviting other trustworthy adults to be involved in their children's lives. You can "adopt" an aunt, uncle, or grandparent. This process has been extremely successful in helping children adjust in a healthy way.

Dependent children feel alienated. They feel like they don't fit in, almost as if they are insignificant to their family and their world. Studies have shown that drug abusers feel similarly alienated. You can help your children move toward a healthy degree of independence by giving them a sense of identity within a social network.

(3) Independent children feel creative and competent.

Children need to feel capable, qualified, and adequate to face the challenges and stress of life. They need to feel they can have an impact on the world around them. To achieve this they need flexibility. This requires parents to encourage their children to use their imaginations. Studies have shown that drug-seeking children are less imaginative, less flexible, and show more rigidity than non-drug seeking children. Encouraging creativity should begin as early as possible in the child-rearing process. In fact, the earlier, the better.

Most children are naturally creative and curious as infants. If we as parents encourage their investigation and imagination, they will usually remain creative. Allowing them to solve problems on their own and then praising their solutions also helps. Parents who discourage curiosity or who are critical of questions children ask will squelch a child's creative skills. Research also indicates that punitiveness discourages a sense of adequacy or competence in children. Parents who avoid using fear or extreme criticalness as a disciplinary tool are more likely to raise children with a healthy sense of completeness.

Children also need to feel adequate to meet the stress of their world. Those unable to cope with stress are more likely to seek "help" through alcohol and drugs. "It calms me down" is an excuse often heard to rationalize drug-seeking behavior. The stress youth face today is indeed significant and far greater than at any time in the history of our world. Children need help in dealing with stress, but the help they need is parental presence and time, not a drug.

(4) Independent children are growing toward self-discipline. It is not easy to become self-disciplined. In fact, it takes a lifetime. Yet, ever so gradually, parents must turn the discipline process over to their children. When parents constantly direct and make decisions, children develop hostile dependency. Many young adults get stuck in the process and remain dependent on their parents, though hostile about their neediness. They can't let go, but are unable to embrace their parents the way they would like. The result is, these youths experience a perpetual cycle involving anger, dependence, inadequacy, and back to anger.

Self-discipline leads to independence. Several studies have shown that drug-addicted teenagers rate low on self-discipline and high on impulsiveness. They earn lower grades, usually as a result of low self-discipline. In reality, many adults never achieve a healthy level of self-discipline. As a result they lead lives of dependence and unfortunately they too often turn to drugs for an answer.

(5) Independent children feel interpersonally adequate. A well-researched study found adolescents who drink regularly have poor interpersonal relationships. They were more belligerent with their friends, got into more fights, and lost more friendships. Many times they reported their drinking was a way to escape the stress of interpersonal relationships. Similar results have been found in studies of other drug-abusing children.

Another intriguing study completed at California State University in San Francisco found "only children" to be significantly more involved in tranquilizer use than children who grew up with siblings. Only children also reported slightly higher use of marijuana, amphetamines, barbiturates, LSD, mescaline, codeine, glue, and nitrous oxide. The reasons why this is true are unknown. Speculation is, however, that without siblings present to practice interpersonal skills, these children become more withdrawn and dependent.

Interpersonal communication skills can be learned in various settings. Unfortunately, most elementary or high schools do not teach classes in this area. However, there are instructional programs and youth groups where formal and informal training does occur. Parents can also work with their own children and teach them to be more interpersonally effective by instruction and demonstration.

(6) Independent children progressively accept responsibility for their decisions and behavior. Many adults have difficulty with this process. Most drug addicts and alcoholics have personality patterns classically defined as "anti-social." The behavior is defined as seriously irresponsible, measured by untruthfulness and unresponsiveness, with a tendency to project the blame for their actions onto others. This process has its origins in the early years but usually is not detected until young adulthood.

Adults know the speed limit, but sometimes we choose to ignore the law. When we do, we must sometimes face the consequences. In this way we are forced to become responsible. Laws are written that way. Nobody forces us to obey them but if we violate a law we pay the price. A similar pattern of enforcement will help children learn to accept responsibility for their decisions and behavior. To learn responsibility they must experience the logical consequences of their actions. Parents can help them understand how consequences are related to cause by giving them the opportunity to take chances, make choices, and realize the natural result. If parents constantly intervene and "rescue" their children from adversity, the children will grow to be irresponsible and believe they can "get away with anything."

(7) Independent children have a clear sense of moral reasoning and the ability to make ethical judgments. If your children are going to avoid dependency and drug use, they will need a healthy conscience. Like several of the previous qualities, this requires time and careful nurturing. Moral reasoning and healthy conscience is not a legalistic, narrow-minded approach to life. Nor is it "black-and-white" thinking. More accurately, it is the ability to make difficult choices and abstract decisions concerning right and wrong in a world filled with conflicting values.

The mere ability to make concrete categorical generalities will not help children in the long run. As an example, many years ago the film *Reefer Madness* circulated around the country as an anti-marijuana effort. The film was inanely global in its claims, saying the drug caused instant insanity, psychotic-like behavior, and was responsible for all the world's problems. If the claims had been accurate, or even reasonable, the tactics may have helped. Instead, it became a joke. Today, the film is popular on college campuses as a tongue-in-cheek comedy. Students have difficulty believing the film actually was intended for serious education.

The problem with a concrete, "black-and-white" approach to decision making is that few things fall into such neat categories. As an example, some adults deal with drug education simply by telling their children "drinking is wrong, and if you drink bad things will happen to you." When the child experiments with alcohol and discovers that nothing terrible happens afterward, the concrete system is shattered, leaving the child with no basis to make distinctions. The same principle applies in making all ethical judgments. Children need to be taught the difference between right and wrong, but it cannot be a simplistic or legalistic approach.

Research indicates that church attendance and church-sponsored youth programs help with this. Certainly church attendance is no panacea, but statistics indicate that children who attend balanced churches regularly have a better sense of moral judgment, a healthier conscience, and fewer problems with drinking or drug use. However, a church that uses excessive fear or guilt as a way to motivate children is more a part of the problem than the solution. These churches do indeed make the problem worse. If the youth program pre- scribes simple solutions to complex problems, my professional experience suggests it will confuse the child even more. The same results have been found in multiple research on an international level. Incidentally, none of the research was sponsored or commissioned by churches.

(8) Independent children have a large pool of healthy peers. Peer influence is indeed the most powerful force in a child's life during adolescent years. The decision of whether or not to experiment with drugs and alcohol will often be made in a peer group. If children have a large number of friends who experiment with drugs, they probably will too. If they have a large number of friends who are problem drinkers, odds are they will be too.

Len Bias is a prime example of the power peer groups place on young people. An unusually gifted athlete, he had strong family ties and attended church regularly as a child. There were various adults to whom he was close, including several coaches. Evidence indicates he had a drug-free lifestyle but had peers who drank and used other drugs regularly. Finally the pressure was too much and he gave in "just this once" to celebrate. We mourn the result.

Peer relationships are difficult for parents to influence. Parents who try to choose friends for their children will likely lose. Friends, however, are usually chosen from an available group—the neighborhood, school, club, church, or organiza- tions to which the family belongs—and parents have some control over this pool. Research shows the more "adult- directed" activities in which children are involved, the better their chance of avoiding drug-abusing peer groups.

Another very wise suggestion made by various child-rearing experts is for parents to make friends with their children's friends. There are a number of reasons to do this. One obvious reason is the better you get to know them, the more you'll know what your children are up to. You can tell a great deal about your own children by observing the friends they choose. It is likely that few other adults are willing to befriend this teenager, so any attempt you make will usually be well received. If you make an effort to get to know your children's friends, it is also likely they will alert you if your own child is having difficulty. This happens regularly with adults who take the time to cultivate such relationships and consider them to be important. Helping your children find a positive peer group is a delicate process, but of vast importance. You will have to go out of your way to make a difference in your children's lives. But helping them achieve independence is worth the effort.

A healthy child is one who is perpetually involved in the process of developing independence. It is a process of both incredible difficulty and immense complexity. Complete independence is probably not achieved during the child-rearing process at all. It takes far more time than the approximate twenty years most parents have. But the vital origins of independence and healthy self-esteem begin with loving parents.

Christie, who had been silent up to this point, smiled. "Newport's pretty bad, all right. We used to drive there to get our stash. I guess there are some kids who are drug free, but those were the preps, and besides, they drank. I mean the Baptist crowd wouldn't have anything to do with people like me anyway. It's a real turn off, John. They want to pray about you and stuff. This one preacher was awful. I always felt like they were judging me. Like I was wrong just for living. For me, drugs was better than that. I just didn't like myself so I think that's how I learned to do drugs. Probably, the way I felt about myself was the major influence of all."

"Where did that come from, Christie?" I asked. "Do you know now what it was that resulted in that lack of self-esteem?"

"Yeah," she answered quickly. "I know now. But then I didn't. My Mom and Dad fought all the time. I never got to spend much time with them. When Daddy was home, they would start. Then it was off to my room. So they finally divorced. Daddy would come see me every three or four months or so. He'd be drunk. Mom was on some kind of medicine. She had a nervous breakdown or something. She worried a lot. I just got depressed or something. The drugs seemed like a way out."

"Sandra, you haven't talked yet," Paul pointed out. "It's your turn."

Sandra looked around the group slowly. Her eyes settled on me. "I guess I'm a lot like everybody else," she began. "Except I was given everything. My parents were super nice to me. Probably too nice. I never wanted for a thing. But then I began to expect life to be like that. You know, for everything to be easy.

"Well, that didn't last long. If it didn't come easy, I figured it wasn't worth having. I was just spoiled, I guess. I wouldn't stick to anything. Just gave up. I never learned to hang in there and work.

"As I got older, things got more difficult. But drugs were easy. They were quick and easy. And I got that instant payoff. Really, the stuff made me feel like I could make it. Like I could do anything. And the dumb thing was, I couldn't do anything when I was bombed. I just didn't know the difference."

She quit talking and began looking around the room again. "Back to you, Dr. B. The spotlight is on you now."

I shook my head. "No. The spotlight is on all of you. This is great. You're going to be in my next book. Just think, you might save somebody's life. You all are great."

"Do we get paid if it sells?" Christie called out. "I want movie rights, okay?"

"Be serial, Christie," I joked. We all laughed as Bennie unplugged the recorder.

Questions for Inquiry

1. What dependent personality characteristics do you recognize in your children, yourself, or any other family member?
2. What is your emotional response to the examples of addicts illustrated in the book so far?
3. Of the eight factors describing independent or healthy children, which are the strongest in your child's personality? Which need nurturing and developing?
4. How does the profile of your child compare with the description of a healthy teenager?
5. On the spectrum of overinvolvement to underinvolvement in your children's lives, where would you place yourself and your spouse at this time? Given the information here, what changes will you make concerning your involvement?

Family or Group Activity

Discuss question four with your family to determine if all the members agree with your assessment. Find out how satisfied or dissatisfied members are in this area. If underinvolvement is the problem, ask each child how much involvement he or she desires and in what areas. If overinvolvement is the problem, ask your children for suggestions as to how you can comfortably, yet progressively, allow them greater independence. Once you've reached agreement as to what the problem is, as a family, decide on goals to alleviate the problem, a plan of action for achieving those goals, and a timetable that will allow you to chart your progress. (Note: this may be more than you can accomplish in one evening.)

Journal Entry

What are your thoughts and feelings about changing your level of involvement in your children's lives? Record these before beginning the planned activity just described. Consider any reluctance, concerns, and logistical difficulties. Next, lay aside those thoughts and consider the long-range benefits to your children, yourself, and your family. After your family discussion, re-enter your thoughts and feelings from your new perspective.

In addition, note how you are progressing with your abstention from drugs. Record your feelings and thoughts about how and why you are doing this. Note what kind of support you are receiving from family and friends while you are doing this experiment.

For Further Thought

Regardless of how deeply addicted to drugs an adolescent may be there is always hope. Even a small positive step by a significant adult can create desirable results. Why, then, aren't more adults taking these steps?

Problem child? I've never seen a problem child. I'm not sure there is any such thing. However, I have worked with a number of problem families.
— *Dr. Clint Phillips, 1978*

5

YOUR FAMILY AND DRUG ABUSE

- How do parents contribute to the problem of juvenile drug abuse?
- How can parents help solve the problem?

The first time I met Barry I was walking down the hallway of a small alcohol drug treatment unit housed in a larger hospital. I turned toward my office, passing several patient rooms enroute. When I looked up, my stomach leaped toward my throat!

Flying through a door, totally airborne, was a large, naked adolescent. In each hand he wielded bananas, as if they were combat knives. His feet touched down only inches from me, and he turned in my direction. Face to face with me, and nearly nose to nose, he let out a long, seemingly unending, mournful scream.

The entire episode probably took only a few seconds, but it seemed to happen in slow motion. By the time his screaming ended, my stomach had returned to its proper place and my mind had considered several options. I noted Barry was clad only in ball-point-penned tattoos that covered his face and neck. Normally such artwork caused great pain, but he appeared to be oblivious. I assumed he was on PCP, and I knew better than to agitate him. I feared that the cadre of staff coming down the hall from the nurses' station might do just that.

"Hi," I said calmly. "I'm John Baucom and I just bet I'll be assigned as your counselor. Let's go in here and talk." As we entered his room I observed his shredded mattress. That explained the feathers he exhaled with every breath. "Oh, I see you're hungry," I joked. "Why not have a banana?" Within minutes he was asleep on what was left of his mattress.

That was how our relationship began. Barry proved to have a good sense of humor, and although he doesn't remember our initial meeting he laughs when he retells it to others. He heard it reported among the staff for several weeks while he was hospitalized. We struck up a good relationship immediately, and later when he left the hospital (against his physician's advice), I remained in contact with his family.

Barry's father was unselfish with his money and provided Barry with every material possession he wanted. As an only child, Barry had been to a prestigious private prep-school and was given new sports cars to drive. He was a bit snobbish and conceited, according to those who knew him personally. His mother constantly intervened when he was disciplined at school and on two occasions, through persistent complaints, managed to get his grades changed.

His father carried a reputation from his early years as being "tough as nails." A contraction of that description became his nickname. He was called "Snails" by his friends and business associates. And apparently he got the name the old-fashioned way—he earned it. Snails was a hard act to follow, both personally and professionally. He simultaneously criticized Barry and overprotected him from others who might make unfavorable comments. He traveled a great deal in his business and had little time to build a close relationship with his son. Regardless, Barry worshiped his father.

Both Snails and his wife smoked cigarettes and drank alcohol regularly. They disapproved of Barry's drug use, however. In fact, Barry's drug problems led to physically violent confrontations with his father on more than one occasion. That didn't prevent Snails from arranging for Barry's "driving while intoxicated" charges to be thrown out of court on three separate occasions. Nor did it prevent him from hiring the best attorney available to get Barry's felony drug charge reduced to a misdemeanor. Certainly it didn't prevent Snails from buying Barry two new cars in a three-year period so the wrecks wouldn't have to be reported to the insurance companies. And unfortunately, it didn't prevent Snails from leaving his son on the company payroll even though Barry had not worked a day in over two years.

"He's all I've got, John," Snails confided to me privately. "I just can't stand to let him go to jail. Somebody would kill him there."

"I know there's no easy answer," I responded. "But you've got to take a stand somewhere. You have to start someday. Give him some motivation to work. Give him a reason to stay straight. Right now there is absolutely no reason for him to quit drugs and go to work. He doesn't have to. You make it easy on him. If I was your son I wouldn't work either. You want to adopt me?"

"I never do right with you, do I?" Snails would soften. "I've never once done what you suggested. But I do try, John. I guess I just can't take a stand like this with my own flesh and blood. . . ."

I thought of my own two sons, and I knew how hard it would be for me to do what I was asking Snails to do.

> *It sounds kind of different to say it now, but I
> really wanted them to draw the line some-
> where. It's weird to think you're in charge of
> the whole family. I mean, I was only eleven.*
> — Janet (age 17) Wilmington

How Do Parents Contribute to the Problem of Juvenile Drug Abuse?

Adults can unwittingly encourage drug or alcohol abuse in children. Certainly there are cases when the encouragement is overt, such as selling drugs to juveniles. The strongest encouragement, however, is far more subtle, and far more powerful. It involves the more discrete observations juveniles make of society at large and of their parents in particular.

Parents, though perhaps unintentionally, often model drug use. A 1974 study revealed that the highest rates of adolescent marijuana use belonged to young people whose parents use over-the-counter drugs on a regular basis. And a study of young people whose mothers used tranquilizers daily revealed that 37 percent of those surveyed had tried marijuana and 15 percent had used an opiate. In contrast, among youth whose mothers had never tried tranquilizers only 12 percent had tried marijuana and a meager 2 percent had used an opiate. Parallel statistics exist among drug-using populations. It appears that parents who use legal, over-the-counter or prescription drugs are more likely to produce children who use illegal drugs.

Another study, sponsored by the Veterans Administration, looked for predictors of success and failure rates of patients discharged from drug-treatment programs. One consistent and accurate predictor of failure was a substance-abusing parent. If the patient had a parent who abused drugs or alcohol, failure was predicted, regardless of the course of treatment in the hospital. In a separate study, at the University of Michigan, a similar result was discovered. This study looked at teenagers involved in drug-treatment programs. Over half of these adolescent addicts had parents who were also addicts.

You know, she tells me I can't do any drugs.
But why not? I mean, she drinks. She even
gets drunk. That's worse. At least I don't smell
like puke when I get high.
— Erik (age 17) Knoxville

We sat in the rustic room in chairs forming a disconnected circle. The vigorous exchange of ideas concerning family life and child rearing stimulated my thinking. Long ago this group of adults had learned to feel comfortable with one another; our honesty and lack of inhibitions led to interesting conversations. We welcomed everyone's input.

"No, I don't agree," one spoke up. "Back in biblical days they used to sacrifice kids. Look at Abraham. He almost killed his son in an offering."

"Well, that's different." Lou smiled. "Didn't he do that because God told him to?"

"Still, he was going to do it. He really didn't seem to show any hesitation about it," another responded. "I'd say society has come a long way. What would you do if you thought God was telling you to sacrifice your child as a burnt offering? I'd think I was hearing things."

"I don't know . . ." Paul hesitated. "I don't think we have come as far as you seem to indicate. We still make sacrifices of our children."

"Not like that," someone said. "We make compromises as parents, but nothing like that. Nobody offers their kid the way Abraham was going to."

"Maybe that would be a safer alternative." Paul looked up seriously. "I think we give up our children to a lot less worthy causes today. You talk about sacrifices. We make plenty of them."

"You're right," Mary agreed. "We sacrifice our children when it comes to a lot of things. Child care is one of them. Time is another."

Paul nodded his head slowly, looking at the floor. "I think we still sacrifice to gods," he began. "But now the gods are just a little bit different. We sacrifice our children to the god of education, the god of medicine, and the god of television. Really, I don't see a great deal of difference there."

I sought Paul out after our meeting. "I was interested in what you said," I commented. "Do you really see it that way? You think we sacrifice our children that way?"

"Yes I do," he replied. "It's frightening to see what we're doing with kids today. I get the feeling most parents have given up. It's almost like they've thrown in the towel. Most parents don't seem to have any idea what to do."

"I guess you talk to parents quite a bit. Pastors must do quite a bit of family counseling."

"Yes," he assured me. "I spend more time counseling families than doing anything else. Actually, it takes more time than I have to offer."

"What do you hear kids crying out for more than anything else?" I asked.

He looked at me silently for a moment. Without changing his expression he uttered two words. "Their parents."

"That's it," I commented, not as a question. "Parents."

"Uh-huh." He nodded his head.

"You're right," I agreed. "I guess I'll go give my own children some of what they need. Thanks for the time."

"Thanks for your time," he responded. "I'm going to go do the same thing."

As I walked away his words echoed in my mind: "We sacrifice our children to the god of education, the god of medicine, and the god of television. . . . I don't see a great deal of difference there." I knew he was right.

It would seem that the increase of juvenile drug abuse merely reflects the problems of adults and a society that invites such abuse. By modeling the current fashion of instant relief from any kind of pain or discomfort, parents unknowingly fuel the fire of juvenile drug abuse. Steadily and insidiously the problem is permeating every corner of our culture.

The American family of "Ozzie and Harriet" vintage is all but extinct, if it ever existed at all. Family life today is disintegrating like a lit explosive. Contributing to this complex problem are the excessive divorce rate and the lack of time parents spend with their children. According to a Penn State study, the average American parent spends fewer than seven minutes per week with each individual child in one-on-one attention. The study measured only meaningful time together and did not include meal time or driving time. Absence of the extended family and the preponderance of two-parent working families have also taken their toll. The parenting role, to some degree, is in default. The child-rearing process has largely been assumed by day-care centers, television, and peers.

Another study found that male adolescents brought up in broken homes were more likely to abuse drugs later than were those from stable, two-parent families. Identical factors are found on an international level as well. A Czechoslovakian study determined internal disharmony in the home to be positively correlated with drug use among teens. The same study also described parental negligence to be an important factor in adolescent drug abuse. Similar results have been found in West Germany, Great Britain, and Sweden.

Universally, parents must parent. Delegating these responsibilities will not keep us from sharing the ultimate consequences. In reality, the responsibility cannot be delegated. It belongs to us all.

> *When I would be hung over, or sick or somethin' from drinkin', Mom would call in for me and copout. She meant well, but I've learned, that made problems worse.*
> — *Lisa (age 19) Ft. Myers*

If a parent is spending less than seven minutes per week with each child, very little positive parenting can occur. As the relationship weakens, parental influence diminishes and managing the child's behavior grows more difficult. The parent, struggling to contain the child, resorts to criticalness in a final, frustrated gesture. This seldom helps.

Research shows that a critical, hypermasculine father typically produces inadequate, dependent children who are more likely than others to turn to drugs as a salve. Another study found a high correlation between punitive parents and young drug abusers. In fact, frequent spanking was found to be directly correlated with drug use in males. Studies conducted as far apart as San Antonio and Sydney, Australia, had identical results. Unsatisfactory relationships between parents and children are reported internationally as significant precursors to adolescent marijuana abuse. Similarly, the quality of relationships with parents was reported as the second most important factor in a 1984 University of Minnesota study. This study investigated marijuana as well as alcohol use.

The pattern described above reflects in many ways the larger evolution occurring in American society. Our materialistic values are not conducive to good child rearing. Our vision, focused firmly on acquiring status and material goods, takes only an occasional rearview glance at the emotional welfare of our children. This focus leads to a condescending attitude toward mothers who stay home to rear children and fathers who turn down job advancement to avoid uprooting their teenagers.

Families contribute to the drug-abuse problem by denying that it exists, by making excuses for the child, and by lying to keep the child out of trouble. This only complicates problems in the long run. "Rescuing" your child does not help and is a prime factor in propelling hundreds of experimental drug users into lives as abusers and ultimately addicts.

Children need to understand, as do adults, that they will suffer natural consequences if laws are broken. One adverse experience or one negative consequence is often sufficient to help a child become more responsible. Similarly, when children are allowed to avoid paying consequences even once, they learn irresponsibility. Parents who make excuses, lie, or cover up for their drug abusing child have become part of the problem. By allowing children to experience the results of their behavior, parents contribute significantly to the solution.

Nobody enjoys watching his or her own children suffer. And allowing them to get fired from a job, make a bad grade, or even get arrested is difficult for every caring parent. But if the child's behavior warrants the response, it's usually better in the long run to allow the consequences. Bailing out allows children to ignore reality. They begin to think they can get away with anything because "Dad will get me off; he always has before. . . ."

Next time the risk is greater and the stakes higher. But the child takes a chance again. "Why not? If I mess up Dad will get me out of trouble. . . ." This cycle spirals, and the result is a family, community, and national tragedy. Eventually, and ultimately, your child will have to pay the price. Allow him to pay it while still young and the stakes still small.

> *I'm seventeen years old and I have never heard my daddy say he loves me. He acts like he loves me. He just has never said it . . . really . . . never.*
>
> — *Kelly (age 17) Pittsburgh*

How Can Parents Help Solve the Problem?

Whether your family has experienced divorce, addiction, or any other trauma, there is hope. There are things you can do to make your child more safe and secure in this stressful world.

The first thing you can do is offer your child love and unconditional acceptance. This kind of love is more than a passive attitude. It is an active process and has nothing to do with material things. It is never static. Good intentions are never enough. Love must be verbalized as well as demonstrated. Children will never know they are loved unless love is communicated. Only you can do that.

Begin with eye contact. Then say, "You know, I really love you," so your child can hear it. Regardless of what you might think, children never get too old to hear those words. A fifty-eight-year-old woman recently described how she tried to get her eighty-three-year-old mother to return those magic words "I love you, too." Unfortunately, for her it never happened. Verbalizing your feelings is essential for the emotional health of your child and possibly for your own. Saying "I love you, I like you, I approve of you" all are important messages.

Physical contact, such as hugs, is another immediate way to communicate love to your child. Decades ago, research demonstrated the vital importance of touch and skin-to-skin contact. Human touch plays a major role, not only in emotional development, but in physical development as well. Physical and expressed love are two key ingredients of the gift of love. One ingredient without the other leaves a less-than-satisfying result.

Unconditional acceptance is proof to children that they are loved. If you consent to love someone you have to be willing to accept them exactly as they are. Psychologist and author Carl Rogers discussed a similar concept in what he described as "unconditional positive regard." His concept emphasized the separateness of the person from his behavior. In Rogers's view, regardless of how undesirable the behavior might be, the person is always okay. An entire philosophy of "helping" others grew around Rogers's belief in this basic value of humans.

Unconditional acceptance means approving of the behaver, not necessarily the behavior. You can love your children and still not like the grades they brought home on their report cards. Your love need never be in doubt or withheld based on performance. When you give unconditional acceptance, your child will never question your love.

"You know, Tommy, I really love you," Mother states. "I think you are a great kid just the way you are, and I think you're smart too. But that makes me wonder about this "D" on your report card. Let's talk about it, okay? I wonder what we can do to help you bring this grade up. I love you just the way you are, Tommy. You're fine. It's this grade I want to talk about."

> *Yeah, sure I know all that. But what difference*
> *does it make? I never get to see him. Well, I*
> *take that back. I did get to see him when I got*
> *busted and when I went to court. Right. You*
> *gotta sell 'ludes or somethin' to spend time*
> *with your dad. What's that?*
> — *Gene (age 16) Columbus*

Children will get your attention, one way or another. It is better for everybody if you give them meaningful attention and get meaningful behavior in return. We all need attention. People who suffer from a lack of it often become ill or suffer emotional disturbance as a result. Children typically do not get all the attention they need. Your interaction with them is the way they socialize your values and culture. The more time you spend with them, the more likely they are to share your values.

Time and attention are the greatest gifts you can offer your child. This has been demonstrated repeatedly. Unfortunately, parents often learn this secret too late for themselves as well as their children.

> *You know, I just wanted to get the heck away.*
> *Momma had too much on her with the little*
> *ones. I couldn't do anything to help. So I*
> *stayed stoned. Nothing bothered me.*
> — *Stan (age 17) Louisville*

One of my good friends is pastor of a large church in a metropolitan area. The demands on anyone in such a position are great, and my friend worked exhausting hours. He began his career quite young and his "workaholic" tendencies impressed his parishioners. However, it didn't impress his family. There was not enough time left over, especially for his oldest son, Tom.

When Tom turned nineteen he decided to join the Army. His father drove him to the reception station from which Tom would leave for basic training. It was a three-hour trip. As my friend reported back to me, it was the longest period of time he and his son ever spent together alone.

"I discovered," my friend sobbed, "that I never knew him. He had grown up and become a man. I missed it, John. It took me three hours to get there, and over six to get back. I kept having to pull over on the side of the road and cry. All my professional life I put everybody—everybody—in front of my family. But no more. I'm not going to sacrifice the rest of my kids."

My friend followed through with his promise. It meant changing the direction of his career. His remaining children needed his attention. Your children need yours. Perhaps you do not have time to give them because of your career. If so, maybe you need to re-evaluate your career.

> *What was that they said in that movie with Paul Newman? What we got here is a failure to communicate—to communicate, right? That's the problem we had. We just didn't have any. Nobody communicated. Not them or me.*
> *— Felicia (age 18) Decatur*

Your children need two-way communication with you. They want to share and to be heard. They need someone to listen, and you are the best person to do it. Most children are not used to having adults listen to them, so they are naturally suspicious when someone listens for the first time. When I first meet teenagers in counseling, I focus on gaining their trust. For the first two or three sessions, I say almost nothing about the reason they came to counseling. Instead, we talk about soccer, movies, music, or anything else the teenager wants to discuss. After talking about these inconsequential (and non-threatening) issues for a few sessions, the teen is more than ready to discuss serious subjects. Time is invested in "small talk" so the child will be more willing to discuss "important talk."

One of the easiest ways to let your child know you're listening is to give feedback. Feedback is a simple, but valuable skill. After listening to what your children are saying "feed back" to them what they just said. Begin by saying, "What I heard you say is . . ." or "You seem to be saying . . ." or "Sounds like you . . ." Then let them know what you heard. End the feedback by asking, "Did I hear you correctly?" This process usually both surprises and flatters your child.

It's also important to communicate with children about coping. Talk to them about the problems they will face or are already facing with peers. Talk to them about stress. Listen with full attention and nonjudgmentally. This is a good way to keep the communication channels open.

Children also need structure. They need to know which behaviors are okay and which are not. They need to know what the specific expectations are for them. There needs to be freedom within the framework, but the structure and boundaries need to be clear. The consequences of breaking the boundaries need to be articulated clearly beforehand. Although some boundaries should remain till children live independently of parents or guardians, they should be expanded with increasing age and responsibility. Within the confines of such a progressively structured environment, a child feels safe to learn responsibility.

Structure can take the form of rules. If you have rules for your children, they need to be in writing along with the consequences for breaking the rules. As an example:

Rule: Turn your stereo off before going to school. Consequence: If you fail to turn your stereo off, you lose it for twenty-four hours.

Most families with children have six to twelve rules. Sometimes these rules are clearly stated. Sometimes they are only implied. Rules that work are usually brief and simply stated. And they have usually been discussed with the children. When an issue arises that is not covered by the rules, make a new rule or write a "contract." Contracts are written and signed agreements between two or more people. A contract is usually in effect only temporarily, for a determined amount of time.

Establishing motivational systems such as point cards or other behavior modification programs is also helpful in managing behavior, especially with younger children or those who need a great deal of structure. Simply put, these systems reward your child for achieving certain goals. Each achievement is rewarded with points, or some kind of token. After points are accumulated the child can "cash" them in for certain privileges or gifts. These systems are usually quite successful and help children learn self-control.

If children are reared in a comfortable emotional environment where they feel confident and safe, the risk of dependence on a drug or anything else is small. If parents or interested adults model a healthy lifestyle and healthy coping mechanisms, the odds are even better that the child will be independent and strong. If parents build a strong relationship with their child, or with any child, that too, increases the odds in the child's favor.

The fact remains, however, that children have freedom of choice. Parents can do every positive thing they know to do for their children and take every possible precaution, and still have a child who makes a bad choice. Drug use is an individual decision. Caring parents can increase the odds that their children will be able to "say no to drugs," but the decision ultimately belongs to the child. And some simply make bad choices.

One evening I received a phone call at home from Snails. A big-name drug pusher had threatened to kill Barry if Snails didn't pay. I was shocked at the thought someone would take that kind of stand with Snails. But I was more surprised at Snails's response.

"What do you think I should do?" he asked.

"I can't believe you're asking that!" I exclaimed. "Your best friend is chief of detectives. What do you think you should do? Snails, this is blackmail or extortion or something. You can't do that!"

"John!" he shouted. "They'll kill him. He's my son. I can't have his blood on my hands like that."

I paused, sharing Snails's silence for a moment, then I spoke. "And where will it stop? What will be next? Kidnapping your wife? Where are you going to draw the line? I know it's not simple, Snails. Love, kindness—they come in many forms. But you're out of my league now. Don't you think you should talk to the chief?"

"I don't know, John." He sighed. "I don't know. He's the law . . ."

I'm not sure what happened after our conversation. I never asked. I do know the result, though. Barry was arrested the next morning by Snails's friend for selling drugs. So was the drug dealer who had threatened Snails. Within three days nine others were arrested in what proved to be a large ring of dealers and manufacturers of illicit drugs. Barry was involved in it all. At this writing he is in federal prison. Snails visits him regularly. I receive occasional letters. Barry seems to have grown up. I think Snails finally let him.

Questions for Inquiry

1. How much time per week does your family spend together as a unit? In what activities: e.g., meals; athletic events; traveling; church attendance; talking; having fun together; other?
2. How much time do you spend per week with each child in one-to-one interaction? What do you think would be your child's response to the same question?
3. When your child is confronted about misbehavior, how confident would he or she be of your love and acceptance even in the midst of your displeasure or anger?
4. How much time do you spend in "small talk" (i.e., free of criticism), building a level of trust, so that your children will share "important talk"?
5. What kind of boundaries have you built for your children? Are they flexible enough to allow for increasing levels of responsibility with age? How firm are you in consistent enforcement? How clear would you say is your children's understanding of the consequences of breaking family rules?

Family or Group Activity

Hold a family forum on the topic of rules. Ask the children to explain what they think the rules are and what they understand to be consequences of breaking them. Ask whether they think the rules are appropriate for their ages and level of responsibility. As a family, redefine or restructure as necessary to be in line with everyone's expectations and responsibilities. Clarify the consequences, then firmly and consistently enforce them.

Request your school-age children to keep a private log book of their own. In it, suggest they note their own personal feelings and thoughts about the family discussions you are having. Ask them to record anything they may yet be reluctant to say in the family or group discussions.

Journal Entry

Consider the following situation and explore your thoughts and feelings about it in your journal. Your family is offered a business opportunity to advance in status and income. It will require a major move in thirty days, which will mean leaving just at the beginning of your teenage son's senior year of high school. What personal values will influence or determine your decision?

Also, update your feelings about abstaining from your chosen substance. When do you experience the least craving for it? The greatest craving? How can you adjust your schedule or activities to reduce the times of greatest craving? What kind of support have you requested from family and friends?

For Further Thought

A group of school children made up a list of activities they would like to do with a parent or as a family. At the end of thirty days, 95 percent of them were unable to mark off having done even one of those activities. What would your child's list look like after the same period of time? It might be worth a test to see.

The greatest obstacle to discovering the shape of the earth, the continents, and the ocean, was not ignorance, but the illusion of knowledge.
— *Daniel J. Boorstin,* The Discoverers

6

OUR SOCIETY AND DRUG ABUSE

- Why is American society so prone to drug use?
- How do social values affect our children?
- What are the primary sources of socialization?
- Who determines our social values?

"I first played around with drugs when I was ten," Dan explained. "I used to sneak cigarette butts out of ash trays and smoke them. When my parents caught me, they would beat the crap out of me, but that didn't matter. They smoked and so did I. It didn't matter how many beatings I got. My older brother was in junior high school and we'd sneak beer and drink it in the woods near our house. I can't believe we never got caught, but we didn't.

"Smoking marijuana came easy. I was eleven the first time a buddy got me to try it. A lot of the other kids were doing it by then and I thought, what the heck? It wasn't much different than getting drunk, but you didn't get sick, so I figured it was better. Really, I didn't get high the first time I tried it. It sort of grew on me. It was like my buddies told me how I was supposed to feel and later I began to feel that way. Almost like learning how to get high.

111

"Nobody had to tell me how to trip on acid, though. The first time I did a lid of acid, I thought I'd lost my mind. It was a weird trip. It was raining outside and I was in the car. When the rain hit the windshield it was like it exploded—each drop burst into flames and it sounded like cannons going off. I was scared and fascinated at the same time. I got really upset when they turned on the windshield wipers. Somehow I got it in my mind they were monsters attacking whoever was shooting the cannons! It all began to sound like the 1812 Overture with the wipers keeping time. It was frightening at the time, but now I laugh. I'm not sure how I ever survived the first time. . . .

"I just wanted to be like everybody else. I was shy. I stuttered. I thought nobody else was as stupid as I was. I later found out I was dyslexic, but then I thought I was just dumb. Everybody caught on to stuff before I did. It was embarrassing. It hurt. The beer, the pot, the other stuff—all made the pain go away. It's really sad. I was a miserable little guy.

"Both of my parents are alcoholics, although they still won't admit it. My dad's an attorney and he was never home. I think it was just an excuse to avoid my mother. By the time he got home, she would be three sheets to the wind. Then he'd start. We used to find them both passed out in the den before eleven o'clock every night. My brother and I would drag them to the bedroom. The next morning it was like nothing ever happened. It was just a way of life. We used to finish off the booze and throw away the bottles. They never knew the difference.

"Joined the Army after high school. I went to Thailand and stayed high for eighteen months. I did real well, too. Went to college after that. Figured I'd get my C.P.A. so I could afford to buy cocaine. Married Stephanie and moved to Atlanta. Worked at a firm there for five years. Probably did coke or something every day down there. Got arrested and then went to the hospital. That's where I met you. . . .

"Been straight now for six years and four months. It's like learning to live all over again. I didn't know there was such a thing as a life without drugs. I had grown up high. I met my wife high. I really didn't even know her. We had to get acquainted all over again. I had even graduated from college high. Everything was brand new at first. The biggest problem was learning to like myself straight. I liked who I was high. I didn't like myself straight though. That was tough."

Why Is American Society so Prone to Drug Use?

It is doubtful that any society has ever been as drug oriented as our own. Drug use is an entrenched part of American culture. From television advertisements, parents, and peers the message is reinforced. Anything—menstrual cramps, tired blood, baldness, loneliness, ugliness—can be cured. For every ailment, real or imagined, there is a magical pill to help. "No reason to struggle. No reason to hurt. Take this. Drink this. It will be better." Chemistry can cure anything. If you have doubts, visit a local drug store. Someone will buy and consume every item you see on the shelves.

And the magic is consumed regularly. Twenty-seven million pounds of aspirin per year; 1.5 billion drug prescriptions per year; laxatives, tranquilizers, painkillers, sleeping aids, etc. "This is a drug society," says psychopharmacologist Dr. Ronald K. Siegel. "We have prescription drugs, over-the-counter drugs, and drugs you can buy in a grocery store. We have to understand that the drive to intoxication is irrepressible, unstoppable. . . ." It appears that drug and alcohol appeal have penetrated the very core of the American value system.

Modern American society has often been referred to as having a "fast food" mentality about problem solving. We demand quick fixes and instant resolutions to complex problems. We have learned to rely on services that provide one-hour photographs and thirty-minute laundry, and drive-through windows that serve instant meals and even dispense prescription drugs. We have grown accustomed to quick cures, quick food, quick marriages, and quick divorces. We do not tolerate pain or inconvenience well. Our society is a drug pusher's dream. He promises a cure for our intolerance. The cure is called escape. And even though its relief is only temporary, we seek it regularly. "Genius," said Galileo, "is eternal patience," but patience is not a commodity modeled to children today.

> When we were in Istanbul nobody ever wanted the stuff. We had marijuana growing in our yard. Opium poppies grew by the airstrip. It was no big deal. But liquor was illegal so that was what we wanted.
> — Chad (age 26) Cleveland

How Do Social Values Affect Our Children?

Children are helpless at birth. The neonate knows almost nothing and cannot survive without the help of others. Different from other animals, the human infant does not possess instinctive patterns of behavior. The human baby is a biological being with almost no personality. Through a long-term, complex process of social interaction, the baby begins to acquire personality and learn the way of life of his society. This is called socialization. It is the link between your child and larger society. Values, language, skills, beliefs, and habits are all learned through socialization.

As an example, a classical study by anthropologist Margaret Mead illustrated how culture influences gender roles. For this study she investigated the habits of three separate primitive tribes of the New Guinea jungle. In one tribe, the Arapesh, Mead found both men and women conforming to what we could call feminine behavior. Both were gentle, passive, and emotionally warm. Aggressive, competitive behavior was discouraged in male and female alike. However, nearby Mandugumor tribe members were cannibalistic headhunters.

Male and female alike were encouraged to be violent and aggressive, and both were hunters. In this tribe both genders exhibited what we traditionally identify as masculine behavior.

The Tchambuli tribe, on the other hand, had strong differences in gender roles. But the roles were opposite of what westerners consider traditional. In this tribe women were dominant and filled more of a provider role. They did most of the hunting and were more aggressive and warlike. The men were more artistic, gossipy, and emotional. They performed the majority of domestic duties, including the nurture of children. In this tribe, women exhibited more traditionally masculine behavior and men showed more traditionally feminine traits.

Mead's study illustrates the deep power of the socialization process. There are no significant biological or hormonal differences in these New Guinea tribes and modern Americans. Yet, there are tremendous differences in the expectations of their culture and certainly in the way those people are socialized.

What Are the Primary Sources of Socialization?

There are several methods of learning. We learn from what we hear in classrooms and from what we read. We also learn from casual conversation. The most effective learning method by far, however, is "modeling." Modeling includes long-term exposure to a way of life, patterns of interaction, and the culture in which we are raised. Continual conscious and subconscious observations make an indelible mark on a child's personality and habits. Ultimately they will choose and adapt some of these influences into their own way of life and their own definition of personality. The primary socializing influences generally fall into five categories: family, peers, school, media, and institutions such as the church. Since other chapters deal extensively with the first two, I've only summarized them here.

In general, the family is the most significant source of socialization. This is true primarily due to the family impact during early childhood years. Children first begin to internalize values and customs by observing and interacting with other family members. Much of the socialization at this level is purposeful and planned, but even more of it is accomplished on a totally subconscious level. Parents and other adults are observed by the hour. The way they behave and interact are permanently imprinted on the child's subconscious mind. As these children approach adulthood, they begin to mimic patterns they observed years earlier without even thinking about it. This includes patterns of drug use. As established earlier, drug users' families were far more likely to be involved with drugs, including over-the-counter and prescription drugs, than were non-users' families.

Peers are also a major source of learning and socialization for youth. Friends have a tremendous influence that increases with the age of the child. As children develop significant relationships outside the family, their appearance, habits, and language adapt to conform with their friends. Conformity and group acceptance is of ultimate importance to the adolescent. The same influence applies to your child's drug-use habits.

School, the third source of socialization, is more than just a platform for formal education. It is also the stage for most interaction between peers, a source of significant adult relationships, and the place where much of your children's informal education takes place. Among the skills learned informally are the importance of responsibility, being on time, and respect for authority other than family. Without a doubt school is a cornerstone of your child's development. It is a powerful factor in whether or not children use drugs. This emphasizes the importance of knowing what your children are being taught, both formally and informally, at school. The best way to stay informed is by maintaining a close relationship with your child's teacher. Most teachers are quite willing to spend time with parents when given the opportunity.

Mass media is the fourth primary source of socialization.

This category includes forms of communication that reach a wide audience. Magazines, books, radio, television, music, etc., are powerful forces in the formation of a child's values and behavior. The average high school graduate will have spent 11,000 hours in an academic environment and 40,000 hours in front of a television during his or her lifetime. Statistics indicate that one out of six television commercials the eighteen year old has observed was selling a substance to "cure" any pain the viewer may be experiencing. Our society both models and pushes drug use.

Although the exact impact of mass media is difficult to measure, there are some indications. Studies and discussion have shown that children often imitate events portrayed in media presentations, often with tragic consequences. For example, over two dozen Japanese teenagers took their own lives after a rock star committed a similar suicide. Similar responses were reported in the United States after the release of the movie *An Officer and a Gentleman*. An increase of suicide was even reported after the airing of a network special concerning the problem of suicide. The special dramatically portrayed the true story of two teens who took their lives in a love/suicide pact. Weeks later the suicide was recreated step-by-step by other teens who had watched the special.

Evidence indicates that frequent exposure to a behavior or an idea leads to a potentially dangerous desensitization. Most of the studies were inspired by the response of several dozen New York City residents who observed a murder and failed to respond. In 1964 a young woman named Kitty Genovese was violently murdered outside her apartment complex. Her attacker took over half an hour to kill her while at least thirty-eight of her neighbors watched the murder from their windows. Not one helped her, nor even bothered to call the police. Subsequently, researchers wondered what caused the observers' apathy. Hypotheses were offered, one being that Americans have become desensitized to violence through constant exposure by media. If we can become desensitized to violence and even murder, as it appears we can, there is a great risk of becoming desensitized to the dangers of drugs.

In addition to desensitization, another danger of the media is that it glamorizes drug use. The drug dealer is often portrayed by the media as a folk hero who lives in the best home and drives the finest car. Another study investigating alcohol use among teenagers who admitted being regular drinkers found that the teenagers were imitating "music heroes," again demonstrating the power of media.

As long as media portrays alcohol and drug use as the best way to deal with life's problems, addiction will increase. The problem will worsen as long as youngsters are insidiously brainwashed that alcohol is synonymous with wealth, sex appeal, and happiness. One of the many paradoxes of our culture is that drug use can be very public, socially approved, and even avante garde, yet treatment for the diseases caused by drug use is a source of embarrassment and shame. I have had several friends who were turned down for insurance policies because they had been treated for alcoholism. Yet I have never heard of anyone being turned down because they drink. Societal values and the odds are stacked against sobriety.

> *There was this dude I knew and he was talking to me and he asked me if I wanted anything. Well, I was scared and so I took it and didn't look or anything. Before long I was tripping with him and we laughed and everything. It was all right.*
> *— Donnie (age 14) Morgantown*

The final group of socialization sources are generally categorized under the heading of other institutions. They include the church and organizations such as Scouts, youth clubs, etc. Studies have illustrated they can be of vast importance. The effect of these sources, however, depends quite simply on whether or not they are used, and most often they are underused. Children who have the fewest problems with drugs generally are heavily involved in activities such as these that are supervised by adults. There are exceptions of both obvious and glaring proportions, but generally this kind of activity is both positive and powerful.

Raising independent, emotionally healthy children takes far more than one or two parents. It is a problem facing all of society. It's not only my child, it's all children. It's not only my small family. It's all families. The problem is not just a community or state or national problem. It is a global epidemic. And it's not just the American family that's threatened. It's the family of mankind. As adults we must reach beyond ourselves to the greater family of all children. They are all my responsibility. And yours.

> *I guess it was just so available. If you didn't do it you could fall way behind. There was no arm twisting or hard kind of persuasion. It was more like, here it is, if you want to get ahead you'd better use it . . . steroids, speed, and eventually cocaine. . . . Most of the athletes I know did it.*
>
> — *Gerald (age 23) Concord*

Who Determines Our Social Values?

One of my former professors decried what he called "the cultural brainwashing of America." He believed our social values were determined and controlled by industrial and corporate giants who benefit financially from our values and subsequent buying habits.

For example, if I believe it's important to my social success to eradicate "ring around my collar" I will purchase whatever is necessary to do so. If I am convinced "relief" is synonymous with a particular antacid I will purchase it regularly. If I am persuaded masculine camaraderie can only be attained by drinking a particular beer with the boys, I will continue to buy and consume that product. My mentor's ideas were far more complex and astute than my simplification, but in essence, those were his ideas. With the constant exposure to advertising we begin to believe the message. Perhaps brainwashing is too powerful a word, but when it comes to drug use his ideas deserve a close look.

Dan, who is now thirty years old and a successful C.P.A., continued his story . . .

"I guess the one thing I would want your readers to know is that this problem is deep and complicated, both individually and corporately. Our entire society has got to change. Look at television. I actually enjoy beer commercials. But I worry about my kid growing up watching them. The people are having so much fun, they look so cool. And that's the message my kid gets. If you want to have fun, drink beer.

"But they don't show the pain. They don't show the death. They don't show the traffic accidents. They don't show the eleven-year-old kid dragging his mom and dad into bed drunk, slobbering, and wetting all over themselves. And they don't show that kid later trying to find somebody who will act like a dad. If you want to be a man, drink this. That's what society believes.

"I can tell you, John. It comes down to this. The bottom line is somebody gets wealthy off all this pain. Somebody got rich because I started smoking cigarette butts in 1960, or whenever it was. Somebody else got rich when I did acid in Panama City. And lots of people got rich when I started snorting coke. That stuff is not of God, I promise you. It goes back to those commercials, and booze is the worst.

"If somebody dies from Tylenol, what do they do? They take the stuff off the shelf. Somebody finds a safety pin in a cookie and the entire cookie plant shuts down. Can you imagine what would happen to the pork industry if somebody ate a ham sandwich and got drunk and had a wreck? There would be congressional investigations. Pork would be outlawed!

"But every day some drunk driver kills another kid. Every day some teenager moves from cigarettes, to booze, to pot, to heroin. Every day some drunk comes home and beats the you-know-what out of his family. Then his kid comes back after the drunk has passed out and drags his dad into bed. Yet it's not only legal, it's a way of life. Society values it.

"Somebody's getting rich. That's the bottom line. Our country has a real problem. And if we don't turn this thing around we're all going down the tubes!

"That's definitely going to be a bad trip."

Questions for Inquiry

1. Which of the socialization influences (family, peers, school, mass media) had the greatest influence in triggering your own drug use (i.e., nicotine, caffeine, social drinking, over-the-counter or prescription drugs, etc.)?

2. Are you aware of the values your child is learning from school concerning responsibility, morality, attitudes toward authority figures, etc.? If not, you might want to arrange time with your child's teacher to learn his or her philosophy and personal attitude about these qualities.

3. How much "drug pushing" are your children exposed to during the hours they watch television? See also Family or Group Activity.

4. What kind of influence does music have over your children? Have you listened with them to gain first-hand knowledge? If not, do so. Then discuss with your child the meaning of the lyrics.

Family or Group Activity

Watch Saturday morning television with your kids. Count the number of cartoons or commercials in one hour that demonstrate drug-seeking behavior.

Also, watch one hour of any major football, basketball, or baseball game. Count the number of suggestions made that cigarettes, alcohol, caffeine, or pills can answer any problem. Notice how many of the "drug pushers" in the commercials either drive fancy cars, wear fancy clothes, or imply that fame, status, and fortune can be achieved through the use of a drug. Discuss your findings with your children.

Journal Entry

Consider your greatest fear concerning a problem your children might have. Explore, on paper, the specific steps you would take if you discovered your greatest fear was true.

Comment again on how you are feeling without your addicting drug. How often have you "cheated" or thought about it? How much money have you saved? Are you remembering to study your substitute goal twice daily and to verbalize that it *is* your goal?

For Further Thought

Think about the mixed message society gives you and your children: On one hand, drinking is required to be socially accepted, but on the other, if drinking destroys your life you're on your own. Some insurance companies illustrate this value by reimbursing people for medication, yet failing to reimburse people for counseling. Other insurance companies refuse to insure people who have obtained counseling, regardless of what it was for. Apparently they perceive getting help as more costly than staying ill. Thus, incentive to get help is, at best, weakened. If the "stay ill" message is not what you want your children to experience, what can you do to change or prevent it?

Our drug problem is the Titanic, and society is along for the ride. Situation is, we're looking at iceberg tips rather than changing course. We gotta quit that, or we'll all go down with the ship.

— Dr. Winford Hendrix, 1985

7

DETECTING JUVENILE DRUG ABUSE

- How is teenage depression related to drug abuse?
- What are the signs of teenage depression?
- How can we detect drug abuse among juveniles?
- What factors influence drug use?

The answering service message indicated I was to call Tom and left a number at which I could reach him. As I dialed I searched my memory for a clue as to who Tom was. Neither the name nor the number was familiar.

"Hello," a husky male voice sang out.

"Hi," I responded. "This is John Baucom. I had a message to call Tom at this number."

"Well, hello John," he drawled. "I know somebody who thinks you hung the moon. Does the name Bob Howard mean anything to you? You don't have to claim him if you don't want to. I wouldn't either, but he's my brother-in-law."

"Oh, I'm sorry he's your brother-in-law," I said, playing along. "We all have our burdens in life; I guess he's yours. I've heard Bob talk about you."

"I hope you didn't believe him. He's a liar and a thief, as I'm sure you're aware . . ."

I laughed aloud at the characterization of my friend Bob. Actually, Bob was a local youth minister, and one of the most reliable and honest people I had ever met. I recalled conversations in which he'd described some of the practical jokes his brother-in-law Tom had played on him.

Tom continued. "Actually, though, I didn't call you to talk about Bob. I guess I should get more serious. I don't know for sure, but I think we might have a problem with our sixteen-year-old daughter. She's been a good kid, and we've never had any trouble with her, but she came in pretty tipsy the other night and got sick. While she was drunk she talked a lot about wanting to die, not liking herself, and being depressed. I think we all need to come in and get some help. Her mom's pretty upset about it, and I just don't know what to do. Can we talk?"

"You bet," I responded. "Let me get someone to call you back and make an appointment."

How Is Teenage Depression Related to Drug Abuse?

Life for many youngsters today has become a series of passive manipulations that result in artificial entertainment and stimulation. Today's world does not demand interaction by the young child. The flip of a switch provides instant entertainment. There's no need to work at building a human friendship when a computer, or even a toy animal, can talk to you. Electronic relationships require neither risk nor struggle. When adolescents discover that all life's challenges are not manipulated as easily as electronic toys, alienation may result. Often the response to this is childhood or adolescent depression. Drug use can be a way of escaping the feeling of alienation as well as medicating the pains.

*Pain. Do you know pain like that? It's like a
dungeon of hell, the loneliness of depression
is. But take a little drink, a little smoke, and
you don't feel it no more. That's it.*
— Ben (age 17) Lexington

One of the few complaints I have with my education is its
incompleteness. My graduate program was one of the few that
taught therapy and change skills, but I had a great deal left to
learn. For instance, I didn't realize quickly enough that
childhood and adolescent emotional problems are far different
from those adults experience. Children are not miniature
adults. Their problems are not miniature adult problems. Their
problems are real, and the pain is real. Their depression is not
miniature either. It is serious and sometimes deadly. It is one
of the most misunderstood and misdiagnosed problems in
adolescence.

Depression is nearly impossible to define on paper. It's a
phenomenon that no one can explain, but everyone has
experienced. Some say it is a mood of sadness, despair, and
discouragement. Others say it is hopelessness accompanied by
reduced activity levels. Some describe it as negative feelings,
painful dejection, having difficulty thinking, and slow physical and mental activity. Perhaps it involves all of the above.
Yet in children and teenagers depression manifests itself
uniquely.

Drugs is everywhere!
— Carrie (age 15) Augusta

Adults who become depressed look it. They appear visibly
discouraged, have a sad, drawn face, and seem generally
lethargic. If you ask a person sporting this appearance what's
wrong, they will usually tell you they're depressed. But with
children and young adults it is different. They do not know
what depression is. Apparently what they experience is

general apathy, a degree of improperly expressed anger, and ultimate confusion. Since they have no understanding of depression, angry expression soon follows. This "acting out" is often misdiagnosed as "rebellion." Children experiencing such mood swings are vulnerable to drug use because they will attempt to medicate the pain and loneliness that accompanies this severe and confusing condition.

Todd is typical of many adolescents who use drugs to medicate loneliness and alienation. The first time we met, we didn't even discuss drugs or emotional crisis.

"Dr. Baucom, this is Todd," the secretary announced as she introduced us the first time.

"Thanks, Jeanie," I responded, and then turned to Todd. "Hi, Todd. I'm John Baucom." We shook hands, and Todd smiled.

"I've heard a lot about you," he said. "My mom saw you on TV, and you've seen some of my friends in counseling before too."

In a case like this, the process of building rapport is much easier. Todd already seemed to have goodwill toward me and counseling. It's always important, however, to build the relationship slowly and to search for common bonds, for things both parties can talk about comfortably.

"Well, I hope your friends didn't say I was weird or anything like that."

"Oh, no. Everybody said you were pretty cool."

"Say, I hear you are in a band and that you write music."

He nodded. "I love music. The band split up a couple of weeks ago, though. But we'll probably get back together. You like music?"

"Sure. I'll give just about any kind of music a chance. By the way, has anyone ever told you that you look a lot like Jim Morrison?"

Todd smiled widely. "Thanks. I've got to grow my hair out a little bit longer and then get it layered. He's one of my heroes. Do you think he's dead? I don't. He was a different kind of guy. Did you ever see him in person?"

Todd was a tall, thin adolescent. His hair and general appearance were much more consistent with the mid-sixties, when Jim Morrison and The Doors were popular musicians, than with the eighties. Although Todd's I.Q. was extremely high, his grades had been slipping. Over the past eighteen months, his A's and B's had dropped to mostly D's. His father, a local college math professor, had a theory to explain Todd's poor grades. He claimed that there is a positive correlation between grades and hair length of teenage males. "As one lowers, so does the other," he asserted.

As Todd grew more preoccupied with music and the band, his friends and habits changed. At one point he even quit eating so he would lose weight and look more like a rocker. "You don't see any overweight rock stars on stage," he later explained to me.

Family conflict increased as Todd's behavior grew more erratic. He began staying up at night to write music. This caused him to doze off in school. He even snored in one class. Todd became defensive and angry when confronted about his behavior, and he began to have severe mood swings.

As Todd's friends and behavior changed, so did his values. Soon he was experimenting with marijuana and other drugs. Hiding his drug use from his parents caused Todd a great deal of guilt. This guilt, combined with the anxiety and frustration he was already experiencing, left him deeply troubled, which made him turn to drugs more frequently. "It was the only time I didn't feel crummy," he rationalized. "It made the hurt go away."

Eventually Todd's father discovered a roach clip under the front seat of the family car after Todd had driven it. This resulted in a major family confrontation, and eventually led them to seek counseling together.

In time, Todd made his own decision to remain drug free. The family made peace with each other, and Todd's grades went back up. His hair remained long, though. His dad's theory was wrong.

What Are the Signs of Teenage Depression?

The following list of depressive symptoms will help you determine whether or not your child is depressed and how severe the depression is. If any of these symptoms occur in combination and persist for an extended period of time, seek professional help for your child. "Shop around" and ask questions until you are sure you have found someone who has special training in working with children.

Early Stages

Inability to concentrate
Excessive daydreaming
Withdrawal from friends
Impulsive acts, seemingly without forethought
Decreasing grades
Change in eating or sleeping habits

Middle Stages

Acts of aggression
Rapid mood swings
Loss of interest in work, school, etc.
Loss of friends
Boredom
Preoccupation with physical complaints
Mild rebelliousness
Sudden changes in personality

Danger Stage

Visible depression
Anorexia
Alcohol or drug abuse
Suicide threats, attempts, or gestures
Giving away prized possessions
Preoccupation with death
Expressions of helplessness
Loss of values

Extreme aggressive behavior
Overt rebelliousness

Drug use is a symptom that something is wrong. Depression can be also. Both depression and drug use may be masking some other pain, but before you can help someone hiding emotional problems you must be able to detect the problem.

> *We rolled one and was going to burn it. But his girlfriend came up. So he gave it to me and I put it in my pocket and forgot it. Couple days later Mom came out and said, "What's this?" I went, "Oh, shoot!" What can you do?*
> — Adam (age 16) Lancaster

How Can We Detect Drug Abuse Among Juveniles?

Detecting drug use is not an easy task. The chart in Appendix A provides some of the observable signs and symptoms, but frequently these signals are missed. You can, however, look at the chart and get an idea of things to look for.

Another approach, though more subjective, may be a more reliable indicator of potential drug abuse. This method looks at the personality, personal habits, and environment of your child. It rates each as a predictor of potential drug use. A questionnaire based on these factors appears in Appendix C. Each factor has been drawn from studies that indicate either dependent personality patterns or outright drug use. The reliability or validity of this questionnaire has not yet been statistically established, so the results should not be considered as an indictment or conviction of drug use. A high score, however, does imply possible or potential drug use.

What Factors Influence Drug Use?

1. *Do the child's parents drink or use other psychoactive drugs?* This is one of the leading predictive factors to

determine if a child will become a problem drinker or drug user. This factor is the most important factor in predicting whether or not a child will *continue* to use drugs or alcohol after experimentation.

2. *Does the child associate with peers who are known to drink or use drugs regularly?* Peers are important primarily in influencing initial experimentation with alcohol or other drugs. Peers will often determine which drug your child will try. Peer influence is not as significant as parental influence in determining whether or not a child will continue to use drugs beyond original experimentation.

3. *Do parents and peers both drink or use drugs regularly?* If parents and peers both use alcohol or other drugs, the child will almost undoubtedly become a problem user.

4. *Does the child's mother use tranquilizers?* If a mother uses tranquilizers her child is over three times more likely to experiment with marijuana than children whose mothers do not use tranquilizers. Her children are also seven times more likely to use opiates and narcotics.

5. *Does the child smoke cigarettes?* Children who smoke are more likely to experiment with other drugs. Although highly debated at one time, this statistic has been found to be conclusive. Tobacco is indeed a gateway drug.

6. *Do the parents regularly use over-the-counter drugs?* This is well supported by research. Children of parents who frequently use over-the-counter drugs are far more likely to use illicit drugs than those who don't. Apparently, this is due to the modeling effect.

7. *Do the parents smoke cigarettes?* The significance of this is due primarily to the modeling effect of learning. Not only are the parents modeling smoking, they are also modeling drug use.

8. *Is there a history of alcoholism or other drug addiction in the family?* There appears to be a genetic predisposition to chemical dependency. A history of addiction in the family increases the likelihood of multi-generational addiction. There may also be modeling occurring in this case as well.

9. *Does the child seem to know the difference between right and wrong and have a healthy conscience?* Research indicates alcoholics and drug addicts have low moral reasoning and at times show no sense of conscience. They are therefore able to avoid guilt and continue their addictive behavior.

10. *Do the child's parents spend time in one-on-one interaction with the child?* There is a preponderance of evidence that indicates the child's self-esteem is primarily determined by the quality of the parent-child relationship. Children with high self-esteem are far less likely to be involved with drug use than those whose self-esteem is lacking.

11. *Does the child complain of boredom?* Research indicates children of low imagination and low creativity are more readily bored. These children are also more likely to turn to drugs for stimulation.

12. *Are family rules, structure, and guidelines articulated and written down for the child?* Children who use drugs are less likely to come from a structured and organized family. Logical and fair rules usually help a child establish a sense of identity and avoid the need for drug use.

13. *Could the child's father (or male role model) be described as hypermasculine?* Research shows that this type of male role model often causes children to feel inadequate, which, in turn, makes them more vulnerable to drug use.

14. *Is the child male?* Male children are more likely to become addicted.

15. *Is the child punished by excessive spanking or other harsh measures?* Research indicates this is a significant factor. One study found children who were spanked an average of three times per week before age ten were far more likely to use drugs as an adult than those who were disciplined in other ways.

16. *Is the child allowed to experience the natural consequences of his/her choices? Is discipline enforced in the home by non-corporal measures?* Although spanking increases the likelihood of drug use, discipline does not. This is especially

true when children are allowed to experience logical consequences of their behavior. Boundaries, structure, and discipline are very positive. Physical punishment, however, is not.

17. *Have drugs, drug paraphernalia, or drug-culture evidence been found on the child's person, room, or clothes?* Most children will eventually leave evidence of their drug use lying around. This is usually found in clothing, automobiles, or bedrooms. Some say this is an intentional, but unconscious, attempt to get help.

18. *Have the child's family or friends complained of money or personal property missing from home?* Children who develop a drug habit are frequently forced to steal to afford drugs.

19. *Does the child appear withdrawn or alienated?* Most teenagers who use drugs appear alienated and describe themselves as distanced from society.

20. *Does the child participate in activities supervised by adults such as clubs, athletic teams, or youth groups?* Children who participate in such activities are less likely to be involved in drug use. Unsupervised adolescent activities are where drugs are more likely to be present.

21. *Does the child have significant adult relationships other than parents?* Children who have a variety of adult relationships are far more likely to avoid drug use.

22. *Has the child been caught telling lies regularly?* Frequent lying is associated with potential drug use.

23. *Does the child attend church?* Church attendance has been found to be associated with an absence of drug use. This evidence was obtained from three different studies, none associated with churches.

24. *Does the child practice self-discipline in areas such as studying, homework, or chores?* Evidence of self-discipline in these areas is significant because it is a good indication of self-discipline in other areas.

25. *Do authority figures in the child's life (parents, teachers, youth leaders, etc.) use fear and guilt as a way of controlling the child's behavior?* Children raised in this environment often seek escape through drugs and alcohol.

26. *Does the child appear to think and make decisions impulsively?* Impulsive children act without thinking and are far more likely to use drugs than those who are less impulsive.

27. *Was the child ever diagnosed as hypertensive or hyperkinetic?* Children with a history of hyperactivity are more likely to use illicit drugs in later life. Apparently this is an attempt to medicate themselves.

28. *Does the child ever exhibit any of the signs or symptoms of depression listed elsewhere in this book?* Depressed children often use drugs to escape the pain accompanying depression. In this way, perhaps the drugs are an attempt at self-medication.

29. *Has the child been observed with dilated or pin-pointed pupils, eye redness, unusual nose rubbing, or persistent coughing?* These are all visceral evidence suggesting possible drug use. This is further described in the Drug Awareness Chart in Appendix A.

30. *Has the child's speech pattern been slurred or inappropriate?* This can be a symptom of drug intoxication.

31. *Has the child exhibited any violent, unpredictable, or bizarre behavior?* This can be a symptom of drug interaction.

32. *Have you observed any poorly coordinated movements such as stumbling or running into objects?* This can often be interpreted as growth spurt clumsiness. However, it may also be a symptom of drug intoxication.

33. *Does the child respond favorably if asked whether he likes himself?* Self-esteem is very important. If the child is able to say he likes himself there is evidence of self-esteem.

34. *Does the child refer to herself in negative terms such as "slob," "dummy," or "nerd"?* These references are sometimes evidence of low self-esteem and a poor self-concept. References such as this should be discouraged by adults and never used by an adult.

35. *Is the child an only child?* Only children are more likely to use drugs. We do not know why this is true. Speculation is that these children are more dependent, more protected by parents, and less likely to build competent communication

skills than children with siblings. All of these factors could lead to increased drug use.

36. *Does the child live in a single-parent home?* Children in single-parent homes are more likely to use illicit drugs. Some indicators point out that children in single-parent homes are more prone to depression and that may be the reason. Also, children in single-parent homes are often less likely to have a large number of significant adult relationships.

37. *Does the child have frequent fights and stand-offs with friends?* This too can be evidence of alienation or depression. The ability to communicate and get along with others is important to remaining drug free.

38. *Is the child in frequent trouble at school, with legal authorities, or other adults?* This can be evidence of drug use, frustration, or depression. The latter two could lead to drug use.

39. *Do adults typically solve problems for the child?* Children must be allowed to solve their own problems to build a sense of competency. Often it is the sense of overwhelming inadequacy that leads to dependence and drug use in later life.

40. *If the child lives in a single-parent home, how often does he see the non-custodial parent?* Nothing affects a child's self-esteem quite as strongly as a parent implying "I don't have time for you" by not visiting. In many ways, it is one of the ultimate rejections.

41. *Is the child exposed to excessive family conflict?* Conflict can lead to excessive stress and a sense of insecurity. When vulnerable in this way the child is more susceptible to drug use.

42. *Has the child experienced any of the following stressful events in the past two years: death of a family member; death of a friend; divorce of parents; moving; lengthy illness (such as mononucleosis)?* Each would leave the child more vulnerable to drug use.

Appendix C lists the preceding questions in the form of a self-scoring test. For guidance in developing a plan to prevent your children from using drugs, answer honestly all the questions and calculate your score. Doing so will show you where you need to focus your attention. Perhaps you can remove the threat of drug abuse by simply spending more time with your child. Or it may require you to reduce or eliminate your own smoking or drinking patterns or other habits. Perhaps a combination of several strategies is necessary.

Tom and his family were all seated in my office when I entered. He stood up and reached out his hand. "Hello, John," he called out. "I'm Tom. You're a lot bigger than I thought you'd be. Shrinks are supposed to be skinny little guys with glasses and pipes. You look more like a football coach."

"Glad to meet you, Tom. And you look a lot younger than I thought you would."

I introduced myself to his wife and two daughters. "It's a pleasure to meet all of you. I feel like I sort of know you already from Bob. He speaks highly of you—except, of course, for Tom," I teased.

"He speaks highly of you, too, or we wouldn't be here. To be truthful, though, we thought about canceling the appointment. But then I decided we should come in just to make sure our thinking is right."

They began an elaborate explanation, filled with details about the family's relationships and patterns. I knew from the way they interacted with one another that they were very close. They sailed together, skied together, and rode bicycles together. Generally, they enjoyed each other's company, and up to this point they had always enjoyed honest and open communication as well.

"We have emphasized the importance of everyone getting along," Tom explained. "We purposely chose family activities that required cooperation, like sailing. We made the girls share a bedroom and a bathroom so they would be forced to get along. Really, there has never been a problem. If anything, perhaps we've been too honest and straightforward. . . ."

Tom went on to describe how he and his wife had been regular drinkers and had never hidden it from their daughters. "If anybody has a drinking problem here it's probably me, not my daughter. She's just following in Daddy's footsteps." He also told me that he had changed jobs several years earlier, which required him to travel a great deal. Before taking the job he had been able to spend much more time with his family. After some discussion he also admitted that the family used more prescription and over-the-counter drugs than they needed.

"So it probably should be no surprise to us that either of our girls would be drinking beer. All you have to do is look at the parents. But we've made a deal. We're all getting on the wagon together. No drinking or drug use unless it's discussed with the rest of the family. It was their idea." He pointed to his daughters. "And we thought it was a good one. So we're all going to cooperate again. If you agree, that is. I'm going to have to change jobs. The girls told me I've been gone too much. It will take some adjustment, but we can make it. So what do you think about our idea? Are we the flakiest family you've ever met?"

I looked around the room. All eyes were fixed expectantly on me. "No," I began, "I don't see much flakiness in this family at all. As a matter of fact, if more families were like yours, I'd be out of a job."

Questions for Inquiry

1. Consider the signs and signals of teenage depression listed in this chapter. Have you observed any of these in your child or another teen that you know well? If so, take appropriate action, as discussed in the following chapter.

2. Based on what you've learned in this chapter, describe to yourself how you think a depressed teenager would look. Have you noticed any of these characteristics in your own child? What can you do to remove or reduce some of the stress in his or her life?

3. Each of the events listed below has been reported by teenagers and adolescent specialists as causes of stress. Familiarize yourself with this list. During these stressful periods, give your children extra amounts of attention and watch for signs of depression.

Death of a parent/family member
Death of a friend
Divorce of parents
Divorce of friend's parents
Broken romance
Excessive family conflict
Puberty
Pregnancy
Romantic difficulty with boyfriend/girlfriend
Moving
Lack of friends
Excessive academic or social pressure
Excessive conflict with best friend
Parent losing/changing jobs
Blending families
Summer vacations
Changing schools
Starting a new school year
Significant national tragedy
Extended illness
Receiving a report card
Receiving a "low" grade
Major exam/test
Losing an athletic contest
Birth of a sibling
Graduation
Leaving home
Media tragedy

Journal Entry

Comment again on your feelings and thoughts related to giving up your addictive habit. What is your level of awareness of how difficult it is to give up drugs? What kind of empathy do you have for those who are already "hooked"? What positive things are happening as a result of giving up your habit: e.g., improved sense of taste or smell, cleaner environment, weight loss, improved rest, clearer thinking, etc.?

For Further Thought

Many parents naively think kids' problems are just "kids' problems" that will eventually go away. By choosing not to spend significant time with teens, parents allow peers and television to exert distorted and inappropriate influence over them. So kids' problems often become complex and uncontrolled. At this point most parents *have* to spend time with teens to try to regain control, establish order, and do extensive problem solving. Actually, many kids' problems are avoidable. So why do you think parents often opt for expensive and time-consuming "cures" rather than methodical "prevention"?

He who only looks at heaven may easily break his nose on earth.
— *Czech Proverb (Circa 1800)*

8

HELPING JUVENILE DRUG ABUSERS

- What are some effective ways to educate children about the drug-abuse problem?
- What is the best way to discuss drug abuse with my child?
- What is the best way to question my child about possible drug abuse?
- How can I know if professional treatment is needed?
- What kind of help is available?

The quality I appreciate most in teenagers is their refreshing honesty. Once I establish rapport with an adolescent, I can depend on him or her to give me honest, straightforward feedback. Sometimes their objectivity is troubling. On more than one occasion I have been informed with total sincerity by "would-be-helpful" teenagers that I need to lose some weight. Others have told me I need to change the way I dress. On other occasions their honesty is flattering. "You know," one fifteen year old remarked, "the thing I like about you is that I can tell you anything and you won't be critical. You'll still accept me no matter what you find out."

I have come to believe that if I don't want an honest answer I should not ask a teenager the question. This assumption *was affirmed during a recent counseling session with seventeen-year-old Bruce.*

"Have you ever experimented with drugs?" I asked.

"Oh, yeah," Bruce assured me. "One time I even tried to kill myself with a bunch of pills."

"Serious?" I questioned. "You really did that?"

"Yeah." He nodded. "I did."

"So what happened?"

"Well, I was pretty upset one night, so I wrote a suicide note, took a bunch of pills, and went to bed. The next morning I woke up and said, 'Hey, I didn't die.' So I found the note, tore it up, and went to school like nothing happened."

I waited a moment for him to continue, then asked, "Well, did your parents find out about it?"

"No."

"Have you ever talked about it to anybody?"

"Nope."

"Why not?"

"'Cause nobody ever asked me until just now."

> *It's nothing but a trap. It's a spider web that you get caught in. The more you fight it, the more you get tangled up. No, it's bad messy. It's worse than a disease. Addiction is death regurgitated.*
>
> *—Jeremy (age 22) Augusta*

What Are Some Effective Ways to Educate Children About the Drug-Abuse Problem?

For years adults have attempted to scare children into not using drugs. Education and treatment programs were similarly based on fear. These approaches have proven to be futile and possibly even counterproductive. Youngsters exposed to these tactics were usually more informed than those presenting them, so school teachers and other adults often lost credibility.

The reality is, most children have observed their parents and peers using drugs for many years with little apparent adverse side effects. Therefore, minor verbal warnings or "horror stories" have few positive results.

Similarly, educational efforts have consistently focused exclusively on the "identified patient," the teenager. That alone makes the process self-defeating. The crisis of drug abuse is far more complex than a simple teenage problem. By isolating children and teenagers we make them scapegoats. Subsequent bitterness may lead to further drug or alcohol use. These approaches have been overly simplistic and often comical. Furthermore, drug education as of 1984 ranked lowest among all alcohol or drug-related funding by the federal government. That value is reflected in the quality of programming attempts.

The most effective approaches to drug education involve the entire family rather than teenagers alone. Recently, some innovative approaches have proven to be helpful. They look at the core of the problem rather than at the surface. I used one of those approaches during a seminar I conducted.

"Who in this room is a parent?" I asked. Nearly every adult raised a hand.

"Okay," I observed, and began pointing. "You, you, you, and the woman in purple over there come up here and form your chairs in a semicircle." The unsuspecting parents began to work their way noisily toward the stage.

"And are there teenagers who belong to these parents? Okay, you stand up too. If you belong to one of these adults, stand up." Several reluctant teens began to rise, rolling their eyes and mumbling. "Don't worry," I assured them. "You get to sit this out." I chose four teenagers from the ones who remained sitting.

I had been invited to the church to speak to the youth group about teenage stress and drug abuse. "No way," I responded to the initial invitation. "Stress is not only a teenage problem. I'll speak if parents also come to the meeting and if you open it to the community." The host cooperated and the turnout was far greater than I could have imagined. Most people, when attending such a conference, expect to be lectured. I gave up on lecturing years ago, especially with adolescents.

"All right," I continued. "Let's get in a circle up here and spread out the microphones so we can pass them more easily. We're going to have a little talk and see if we can all learn something. One of the issues I was told to address tonight was drug use. It didn't specify whether it was adult or teenage drug use, but let's talk about it."

I got the idea for this approach in 1973 while working with teenage drug addicts. In what was then an experimental approach, we decided to use a multiple family group therapy setting. The teenagers were sent to our center by the juvenile court, and continuous counseling sessions were part of their probation. The influx was so great that we were forced to use the multiple family setting.

The group consisted of four to five families sitting together and discussing relationships, drug use, and conflicts. One result that I didn't expect was the continuous dialogue that occurred between parents and children of different families. It was as if they worked at the problems of their own families by proxy. On many occasions the session resulted in an emotional climax as adults and youth resolved their conflicts and renewed their closeness. Family dialogue often continued for days after our bi-weekly meetings.

I used the multi-family format for years in therapeutic settings, and twelve years later began using a version in my seminars. The feedback I got through combining this with a mini-lecture indicated it was a much more effective way to teach. The interactions were spontaneous and real.

After everyone was seated and had made a name tag, I turned to the audience and began speaking. "You all probably thought you were going to listen to someone preach at you, didn't you? Well, not tonight. This is real. You never know what's going to happen. But we're going to sit up here and talk for a few minutes. I will make periodic comments and afterward I will make more structured comments. So you all just listen in and learn."

I turned to my small group and began speaking. "Okay, here's what we're going to do. The adults are ambassadors from the adult culture. The teens are ambassadors from the adolescent culture. We're here for a summit meeting to discuss the peace initiative. I am the chief arbitrator and negotiator. One of the big items on the agenda is drug abuse."

Research shows that this kind of small group format is extremely effective as a way to educate both teens and adults. It also succeeds in opening up communication channels. An added advantage is that other people get to watch and learn vicariously. In fact, a study completed at the University of Florida indicated that small-group learning was the only effective approach to drug-abuse education. By including objective adults in the small group the rapport and awareness is made far more effective.

Any successful drug-education program will involve parents and other adults. In Atlanta, children caught using drugs are placed in educational programs with their parents. Parents are required to attend or their children will not be readmitted to school. Last year 700 students attended the program and only 25 percent of its graduates got into trouble a second time.

Another component of success is reaching youngsters as early as possible. In Massachusetts, some programs are initiated as early as preschool and kindergarten. One police official stated, "If you wait till first grade, you've waited too long."

A third aspect of successful educational programs is perpetual coverage. They are not limited to only one week. Constant reinforcement is the only way to penetrate the child's core value system, which is essential for successful drug prevention. Drug use is currently part of that value system. If youth drug use is going to change significantly, the value system must change. When children learn to "spell relief" correctly, the drug-abuse problem will disappear.

*Really, I didn't have any reason to be alive. I
never really had a place, or purpose, or
anything. It was sort of like being along in life
for the ride. Getting high made me special.*
                                    — Bryan (age 17) Lincoln

What Is the Best Way to Discuss Drug Abuse With My Child?

Surprisingly, drug abuse is a subject that can be discussed on a low-threat basis. News headlines and stories present numerous opportunities to initiate objective discussions that don't require threatening personal involvement. The key to success in such conversations is to remain rational, as did the father depicted in the following illustration.

"Hey, Johnny, did you hear that report on the news today about the drug bust?" his father asked.

"Yeah," replied fifteen-year-old Johnny. "Could you believe it? Right here in dull old Fruitport."

"If we've got drug problems here, that stuff must be everywhere. Did you know any of those kids who got arrested?"

"Nope," Johnny answered. "One of them was a student at school, but I didn't know him."

"What would you do, Johnny, if someone tried to sell you stuff like that? How would you deal with it? What would you say?"

Conversations like this can be frequent and ongoing if parents can remain non-accusing and uncritical. Asking "What if . . ." questions can also be positive if not overused. Obviously though, if parent/child communication is limited to discussions concerning drug abuse, the child will soon become suspicious.

Another useful activity is a role-playing exercise in which the child rehearses "saying no." This gives children practice in turning down drugs. Some families have gone as far as having "dress rehearsals" with one parent playing the part of the drug pusher. Nancy Reagan has used this approach on an almost global level, and the results have been encouraging.

The higher your child scores on the questionnaire in Appendix C, the more important this type of discussion and activity are. And in all cases it is necessary for parents to remain rational.

The natural tendency is to overreact emotionally to what you fear is occurring, but an emotional response will be of absolutely no benefit. It is much better to respond calmly, even if you have to rehearse several times what you plan to say.

When preparing for these conversations, keep several things in mind. (1) *Do not begin the interaction by assuming the worst.* It is unwise to accuse your child of being involved in illicit drug use. If you rely on the accuse-and-question approach, your child will become defensive and you will lose all hope of healthy conversation. (2) *Begin the interaction as a conversation, not as a lecture.* This was illustrated earlier by the father discussing a news story. (3) *Be certain you are well informed.* This is especially if you intend to discuss technical information concerning certain drugs. Children today are well educated about drugs and cannot be manipulated by scare tactics. If your information is inaccurate, your credibility will be lost. (4) *Admit any negative habits of your own, such as drinking or smoking.* Self-disclosure is a good way to gain trust and start a dialogue rather than a monologue. (5) *Ask yourself if you are willing to give up your own addictive behavior, no matter how inconsequential or insignificant it may seem to you.*

What Is the Best Way to Question My Child About Possible Drug Abuse?

The bad news is, the odds are better than fifty-fifty that your child will eventually experiment with alcohol or other drugs. The good news is, most children will not become addicted or problem users. And for those who do, help is available.

If your child scored extremely high on the questionnaire, or if you have found physical evidence of drug use, it is important that you discuss your findings. The same guidelines mentioned earlier apply in this case as well, except calmness and rationality are even more important. In addition, you must remain totally factual. Avoid mentioning fears or suspicions. It may help to list ahead of time the things you have noticed and to go over them in total fairness. If you think you may be unable to be totally objective and fair, find someone detached from the family to coordinate the meeting. Finally, make sure the goal of your discussion is to find a solution, not to accuse or condemn.

After discussing with me their suspicions that their son was experimenting with drugs, Joe and Betty decided to talk about it with him. To avoid arousing his defense mechanisms, they decided to speak to him alone and to try a low-key approach. They rehearsed the conversation several times. Then, with much apprehension, they brought it up during supper.

"Son," Joe began, "we were reading a magazine article the other day [which was the truth] that said almost all teenagers will experiment with drugs or alcohol before completing high school. How do you feel about that?"

Joe Jr. looked at both his parents before responding. "Yeah, Dad, I suppose that's probably true. It's real common to try stuff out today. Didn't both of you try drinking when you were teenagers?"

Joe looked at Betty while clearing his throat. "Well, Son, uh—quite frankly—yeah, I did. I don't know about your mom, but yes, I drank a time or two when I was in high school." Joe looked toward Betty for help. She broke eye contact and began wiping her mouth with a napkin.

"Yes," she finally said. "Yes, Joseph, I did indeed take a drink of beer as a teenager on one occasion, but I didn't abuse it. I took one sip, and that was it until I was out of college. I didn't let it affect my life."

Joe Jr. looked at both his parents curiously. "So are you wondering if I've been drinking?" he asked bluntly. Without waiting for a response he continued. "I have tried beer. Never mixed drinks. And I have tried smoking a joint, but I didn't like it. Mostly I did it to find out what it would be like. Really, though, I have been wondering about you two."

"What?" Joe asked. "What do you mean?"

"You guys drink an awful lot of coffee. Don't you know that stuff is addicting?"

> *I'd tongue my antabuse and go out and party anyway. You can smoke all the weed you want, on top of antabuse. So it don't matter. But I'd tongue it and that way I could drink too.*
>
> — *Chris (age 17) Carlsbad*

How Can I Know if Professional Treatment Is Needed?

Severe addictions become obvious. A child who becomes addicted or persistently abuses drugs will soon be noticed. Dependent behavior, described earlier, or the signals mentioned in Appendix A will help you detect addictive behavior. When children are unable or unwilling to cease using drugs or alcohol on their own, they need outside help.

What Kind of Help Is Available?

As mentioned earlier, the most effective type of help involves the entire family, rather than the child alone, in the "helping" process. And most experts agree that the best help is that which will least disrupt the child's life. If that type of approach is unsuccessful, more dramatic measures may be necessary. The most successful help is provided by such groups as Alcoholics Anonymous.

In 1935, a stockbroker named Bill W. hit bottom. Several years earlier he had lost his livelihood in the stock market crash. Afterward he sought solace from liquor. "Dr. Bob," a friend and physician, spoke to him on several occasions about his health. After going through what he called "a spiritual experience," Bill revisited Dr. Bob. They talked for several hours about how discussing the problem seemed to help. That day they formed Alcoholics Anonymous, a self-help group composed of recovering alcoholics.

Dr. Bob believed alcoholism is a disease similar to a bad allergy. Although it cannot be cured, it can be controlled indefinitely through abstinence. This basic philosophy has continued within AA circles and is probably partially responsible for the program's success. AA is not "treatment" and does not use professionally trained counselors or therapists. It is a self-help organization that supports and encourages abstinence. It replaces drinking peer groups with a sober alternative. Some AA groups even have dances and meals together. This is tremendous evidence to the power of peers, even in adults.

There are probably several reasons groups such as AA are successful. First, members have a thorough understanding of the problem. "It's difficult to con a con." Members are not allowed to manipulate or play games in AA. Groups are also highly motivated to help themselves by helping others. Both the helper and the one receiving help receive benefits.

Equally important are the non-drinking role models provided for new members. Abstinence is a core value of AA and is rewarded with both verbal and symbolic recognition. "Chips" representing length of abstinence are awarded and sobriety birthday parties are celebrated regularly. Members are also encouraged to work through an arduous "twelve-step" program. And the twelve steps stress "work," actually doing what the steps say, not just reading or believing them. This is a vigorous, threatening task for some people, especially steps four and five. Step four requires the alcoholic to take a "searching and fearless moral inventory of one's self." As alcoholics make lists of things, people, and institutions at which they are angry or have resentments they often end up looking objectively at their own character defects, as they see how they've hurt other people. The process, though threatening, is extremely worthwhile. (The twelve steps are listed in Appendix D.)

AA is a good place for you to start if you think your child needs help. Most cities have special groups for juveniles. Al-Ateen and Al-Anon are also provided for family members. Children willing to attend AA and "work the program" faithfully, will probably achieve sobriety. Some, however, may need more intense treatment.

There are almost 10,000 treatment centers in the U.S. alone that specialize in treating addictions. The number has grown so fast that addiction treatment has become a $3 billion per year business. Unfortunately, there is almost no way for a lay person to distinguish between high quality treatment facilities and those established solely for economic reasons. Reports have flourished of some facilities whose interest is more commercial than therapeutic. Yet this should not rule out nor discourage parents from seeking professional treatment. Most communities have several facilities from which to choose. If you carefully and thoroughly investigate the facilities before making a decision, you should be able to find a place that can help your child.

Among these are medical hospitals, halfway houses, residential treatment centers, and therapeutic communities. Some sponsor both outpatient and inpatient programs. Outpatient care is less intense than inpatient and as a result often requires a longer time period. If the child can live at home with no major problem, outpatient treatment may be sufficient. However, if the addiction is severe, inpatient care will usually be recommended.

> *Help me? Help me! You don't even know me.*
> *How you gonna help me?*
> — Lauren (age 15) Arlington

Inpatient facilities have programs ranging in length from a month to two years. These programs usually include individual counseling, educational classes, intense group therapy, and family counseling. Most programs also include elements of AA philosophy. The average length of stay in adolescent programs is six weeks to three months. These programs are difficult for the youngster and the family, but there are few alternatives when addiction is severe.

If searching for such a program, consult several independent specialists for their opinions to enable you to make wise comparisons. Clergy members often have more experience than counselors in referrals of this sort and can be extremely helpful. AA chapters are also a good source of referrals.

Some programs specialize in treating juveniles. Others have totally inadequate programs for youngsters. Treating juveniles is far more difficult than treating adults, and it requires special training. To find an appropriate treatment center for adolescents, therefore, requires special inquiry. Unfortunately, the profitability of treating chemical dependency has attracted some investors whose motive is profit, not helping people. For this reason alone it is wise to screen programs thoroughly. This is especially true with adolescent programs.

The National Institute on Drug Abuse has discovered that adolescents who enter drug-treatment programs have a variety of problems. The problems are complex, usually involving far more than simple drug abuse. They include serious family difficulty; multiple drug-use patterns; psychological or emotional problems complicated by learning disabilities; and often stress-interrupted adolescent development. Drug use is often a cover-up of more severe disturbance. As drug use worsens, however, it becomes a problem of its own, while remaining enmeshed within the larger system.

Research indicates that successful treatment programs must include the family and help the juvenile rebuild his or her self-esteem. Without group therapy, family therapy, and rebuilding the peer group as AA does, no inpatient program has been able to claim honest, long-term success.

Therapeutic communities are long-term treatment programs that specialize in working with hardcore drug addicts. Communities such as Synanon in Santa Monica, California, and Phoenix House in New York rely on a great deal of confrontation in their treatment. Unfortunately, only about 20 percent who enter the program remain the entire length of treatment. Those who do, however, are forced to face the things that prevent recovery—denial, rationalizations, and dishonesty— and many overcome them. Although the actual success rate is difficult to measure, Phoenix House graduates are reported to have a 76 percent rate of abstinence five to seven years after graduation.

Treatment begins with the family. If you need objective help, contact the nearest AA group and speak with one of its representatives. Beyond AA lie a series of treatment alternatives. Most are costly and require thorough investigation. If you think your child needs intense, inpatient treatment, consult several professionals not associated with a specific treatment center. Discuss the decision with a clergy member. It is not an easy decision to make. But for severe levels of addiction, good inpatient treatment followed by outpatient counseling and AA offers the most hope for recovery. If addictions are not treated during adolesence, they will continue into adulthood. In that case, more drastic measures are necessary to get a person into treatment. My meeting with the Johnson family illustrates what happens.

I looked around the crowded room at nine other people. Four were scrunched on the couch together. Others sat in assorted chairs. I dodged a toddler and headed toward an empty seat in a nearby corner.

"Hey there." I reached down to pick up the youngster. "What's your name?" The little boy smiled and patted my cheeks with his tiny pink hands.

"That's Kenny," an unidentified female voice spoke up.

"Well hi, Kenny." I lifted him toward the ceiling. "My name's John. You're sure a friendly guy."

"He loves attention!" The same voice spoke up. I looked down to see a smiling face staring in our direction.

"You must be his mother," I guessed. She appeared to be in her mid-thirties. Her jet black hair was combed straight down to her shoulders. Slate-rimmed, tinted glasses made her hair appear even blacker.

"Yes, I am." She stuck out her hand. "I'm Jenny Johnson. I'm sorry about Kenny. I started to leave him home, but I was told you wanted to see everybody together, and he's part of the family."

"Don't apologize. I'm glad you brought him. I do like to see the whole family and it looks like you've got quite a few folks here."

Jenny began to introduce everyone. "You already know Father McMahan," she began. "He set up the appointment. And you've met Kenny. This is Terry, our daughter, and that's Billy. He's our oldest son. And of course you already know Gary, Bill's supervisor."

"Billy, how old are you?" I asked.

"Eight," he answered shyly.

"Are you scared about being here?" I questioned.

"Uh-huh." He smiled.

"Well, you don't have to worry," I teased. "I'm not going to give you a shot or anything. I'm not one of those kind of doctors."

"That'll make him happy. He hates shots." Jenny looked at Billy and smiled. "Let's see," she continued. "This is Jack, my husband's brother, and my parents are over there...."

The family had gathered to discuss their concern about Jenny's husband, Bill. His drinking problem had grown to almost devastating proportions and had begun affecting him at home and on the job. Bill had been suffering blackouts, concentration problems, and personality changes. On one occasion he disappeared for several days and reappeared as if nothing was wrong. "I just left for a few days," he rationalized. "No big deal. It could happen to anybody."

Bill was a very likeable person and a successful business-man. "But he's slipping," Gary had commented. "He's missed deadlines. I get calls from customers. Everybody is noticing it. The customers like Bill. They're just worried about him. And we've lost three accounts in the last two months...."

Bill had spoken to Father McMahan on several occasions, with little lasting effect. The priest had suggested to me the possibility of a confrontation, forcing treatment in a residential setting. "Outpatient will never be successful," he predicted. Everyone agreed with his recommendation.

This type of confrontation usually ends up as one of two extremes—either very successful or painfully negative. Due to the high risk involved, we would rehearse the meeting in detail until I was satisfied. I stressed the importance of emotional objectivity, to the point of being as non-emotional as possible, during the actual meeting. The participants had brought notes and documentation of past incidents.

"My role is only that of a facilitator during the meeting," I explained. "You have the burden of getting through his denial. The only way to do that is by being totally objective. If you get upset, you lose. Bill will be upset enough for everybody." The first rehearsal went well, but indicated the need for further practice. The second rehearsal went better. The actual confrontation with Bill took place two nights later.

Bill marched stiffly into my office without looking up or to either side. He took a seat and stared at the wall.

"Bill, I'm John Baucom," I began. "And we're here—"

"I know precisely why we're here," he snapped. "I know what you want!" His face reddened as he turned to his wife. "How dare you embarrass me like this in front of Gary. Do you know what this does to my job?"

"Bill," I interrupted calmly. "We're here to talk and we'd like you to listen for a few minutes. Then you'll get your chance. I do want to say, though, that this was not your wife's idea. I have worked with your company for several years, and Gary and I have worked on a number of projects together. This is a corporate meeting. This is a company decision."

Bill looked toward Gary for verification.

"He's right, Bill." Gary nodded. "John works directly with us on these issues. This is a company meeting."

"Well!" Bill retorted sarcastically. "I guess you have me right where you want me, don't you Mr. *Doctor* Baucom," he

sneered. "So just go right ahead with your kangaroo court here.
I'm the accused. Are you going to read me my rights, *Herr
Doktor*?" Bill glared at me, enraged.

"Bill, we're all here for a reason," I began mechanically.
"These people love you. They each have something to say.
They are going to talk to you. I want you to listen and not say
anything. I'll give you a chance to respond later. If you begin to
answer, I'll ask you to restrain yourself. Gary, why don't you
begin?"

We were embarking on what was actually a last resort. Bill's
addiction had progressed to the point that his life was in
serious jeopardy. His entire social support system had gathered to confront him with his behavior. We were also going to
press Bill to enter a residential treatment program. The
pressure and tension in such a meeting is tremendous. After
my original training in conducting such sessions, I had
nightmares that I was being confronted in one for some
unidentifiable problem. The dreams were incredibly frightening, as I'm sure the actual sessions must be. I envied neither
Bill nor his family. The intensity built as Gary concluded his
list.

"So in all, Bill, you've cost the company almost 23,000
dollars over the course of a year, just in two accounts. The
complaints are piling up. And it's all due to your drinking. It's
a real problem."

"Hey, Gar'," Bill began. "Come on, man. It's not like you
paint it—"

"Bill, you'll have your chance to respond in a few minutes,"
I assured him. "Jack, you go next."

Jack, Bill's only sibling, was two years younger. Their
parents were dead. Jack had admitted having a drinking
problem years earlier but had gotten help through AA. He had
also confided that their father had been a life-long alcoholic.
Bill had never admitted that to anyone, including Jenny. In
fact, Bill had been abused by his father regularly during his
binge drinking episodes. This was another factor Bill had
hidden from his wife. Some researchers deny the genetic

components of alcoholism. Yet, through the years I have observed a link time and time again.

"You told me to meet you at 4:00 P.M. You never showed up," Jack read from his list. "The next day when I called you, it was like you thought I was crazy or something. Like the appointment didn't exist. I figured maybe you were right. But the next week it happened again. . . ."

From all evidence, Bill was in the advanced stages of alcoholism. He was already suffering blackouts and memory lapses. His tolerance had decreased. He was drinking in the mornings now. I recognized his reddened face, puffed nose, and bloodshot eyes as common symptoms of chronic alcoholism. Most likely he was suffering the beginning stages of pancreatitis, gastritis, and liver cirrhosis. He smoked spastically as he listened, and nervously lit another cigarette before finishing the first. Several times he leaned forward as if to speak but stopped himself. Instead he rolled his eyes and shook his head, passing the smoldering cigarette from hand to hand.

Jenny's parents went next. Then Father McMahan, the priest who had been the first to contact me. Jenny had gotten Gary to call later. That was when he had suggested we all get together for a discussion of the problem. As Father McMahan began to read, I glanced at my watch. An hour had passed. I usually plan at least three hours for these meetings with a group this size, but sometimes more is needed. I had let the family choose what options they would give Bill. In this case, they were willing to draw the line. Bill would either agree to enter treatment or risk losing his family, his job, and his support group. It was going to be tough.

After Bill's five-year-old daughter cried softly through her list it was Bill Jr.'s turn. I knew he and Jenny would have difficulty remaining calm through this part. Father McMahan had strategically sat between Jenny and Bill Jr. to offer support to both. This would be the most difficult thing the eight-year-old boy had ever been asked to do.

"Daddy," he began reading, "you've always been my hero—"

Bill Jr. was interrupted by his father's first deep sobs.

"My God!" he screamed. "I haven't hurt you, too! What have I done?" Bill began to cry rhythmically, jerking as he sobbed, unable to hold back any longer. I felt sorry for him, but didn't allow myself to join the others as they all cried. Jenny kneeled beside Bill and wrapped her arm around his back.

"We know you don't want to hurt us," she cried. "So let's get help, Honey. Let's save our family. Let's save our marriage. Oh God!" she cried louder. "I love you so much. Save your life! Get help for you and us, before it's too late."

Bill looked down at Jenny and took her hand. "I'll do it," he submitted. "Take me right now, before I change my mind. I feel rotten. What have I done to my children?" He continued to sob openly.

Arrangements had already been made. Jenny had brought his packed suitcase and the admissions clerk had been notified. Bill entered treatment for alcoholism the same day. Six weeks later he was discharged. He has been sober for over three years.

The confrontation was harsh. They always are. I think each one I lead takes another year off my life. But the illness is also harsh. The pain it causes children like Bill Jr. is harsh. And the death caused by cirrhosis of the liver is harsh.

But healing is sweet. With each "recovery" my lost year is handed back and multiplied. A family is restored. A life is given another chance. Miracles still happen!

> *No, I hated being in treatment. I hated it! But I like being straight. I tried on my own first. Treatment did it for me, but I hated it. Yeah, it was worth it in the long run for sure.*
> *— Don (age 19) Riverside*

Treatment of addictions has shown more positive results over the past few years. Many experts claim the chances of recovery have increased markedly. This is especially true if treatment involves the entire family. The view of addiction as an illness is growing. Problem drinkers and drug abusers are viewed less as criminals and more as people in need of treatment.

Help is available and can be profitable to juveniles, families, and society. If we all support drug-free lifestyles and responsible attitudes toward drugs, our values will change. And when our values change so will our children.

Common sense is often uncommon. And so it surprises many to learn that there is actually little mystery to dealing with a child suspected of using drugs. Communication is without question the key. Bruce was a good example. Once I had established trust and a sense of rapport with him, he was willing to talk about anything. I emphasize "trust and rapport" because without these a child will be afraid to communicate honestly about sensitive matters. Many people have asked how I build rapport as easily as I do. I respond honestly and admit, "I don't know. I just try to be myself."

Perhaps no one talked to Bruce about his drug use before our session. That quickly changed, however. With Bruce's permission I invited his mother, JoAnn, to discuss the events in Bruce's life that he had told me about. She was shocked. Simply asking Bruce about his behavior had never crossed her mind.

During the next few sessions I apparently used the term rapport *several times. Finally, exasperated, JoAnn blurted out, "What is it and where can I get some?"*

I tried to explain that it wasn't a commodity, but a sense of emotional warmth and trust.

"That's too vague." She shook her head. "Give me something concrete. Give me a formula I can use."

This type of request is something I have a difficult time with. I detest simplistic, superficial answers for solving complex relationship problems. But I realized there was validity in what JoAnn was saying. After thinking about it a few days, I decided to make it as easy as ABC. During the next session I gave her the following list:

Accept the child *unconditionally*. This provides the child with the needed security that will promote emotional growth.

Be caring. I don't think you can fake this. You either care or you don't. This is "love in action."

Communicate. Keep the channels open.

Don't push. Children today have enough stress. Pushing will only cause more problems.

Esteem your child as an individual. Each child is unique and deserves to be respected for his or her differences and treated accordingly.

Find time to spend with your children. It's the greatest gift you can give them.

JoAnn tried the ABC's and decided they worked. "Only one problem," she said, crossing her arms. "We need G through Z too!"

Questions for Inquiry

1. If your child broke a leg or cut an artery you'd get him medical treatment. If you discover he is involved with drugs, will you get him professional help?
2. In what ways do family and friends hinder alcoholics from getting control of their lives? In what ways can they help?
3. In your community, what facilities are available to help a chemically dependent person? What types of treatment are offered at each one? If a member of your family needs professional help, which one(s) would be appropriate?
4. Who in your family or circle of friends do you think has an alcohol or drug problem? How are you helping or hindering this person's recovery? Would you be willing to be part of a support group in order to help?

Family or Group Activity

If you know of a chemically dependent person in your family or circle of friends, consider the possibility of getting all concerned persons together for a meeting. Discuss what is necessary to save this person from dependency. Consider all options, including what professional services may be needed. Discuss what the network of friends can do to help the addicted person. DO NOT, however, confront the person. Follow through to obtain needed professional help.

Journal Entry

What are your thoughts and feelings about considering a confrontation? If necessary to save a life, would you participate? What are your thoughts and feelings about being confronted if you are a chemically dependent person?

Also, what adjustments are you making to life without your drug of choice? Do you feel in control of your addicting habit or do you feel controlled by it?

For Further Thought

The drug problem in our country is out of control. Efforts by government and private groups have made little if any dent in the problem. If any group of people in our country *could* make a dent, it is a collection of parents and other adults who would be willing to change their own behavior. Why do you think so few parents and adults seem interested in sacrificing their drug-modeling behavior? As a member of this group, how much effort are you willing to invest for the future of your children? What can you do to convince others of the need to change their behavior?

The real question is, what do we do next year?
— *Congressman George Miller, California, 7th District*

9

WHERE DO WE GO FROM HERE?

- Why is drug awareness at an all-time high?
- What are the trends in drug abuse?
- What are the trends in drug prevention?

"I got a contract out on me," Billy Lee explained. "That's why I'm in here. I figured this was the only safe place other than leaving town. Nobody's going to make a hit on me in a hospital."

It could have been one of his grandiose stories, or the truth, or somewhere in between. Billy Lee Thompson was a drug dealer who had recently been admitted to a drug rehabilitation center where I worked. His drug screens had consistently turned out negative, and he had told me several times he didn't use any drugs at all.

"Don't like the stuff," he insisted. "I'm a businessman. That's why most of these idiots go down the tubes. They stay high all the time. Not me, I want to get ahead."

My experiences with Billy Lee Thompson turned out to be an education. He talked freely and learned to trust me. At times he was entertaining. At other times he was frightening. I'm almost embarrassed to admit it, but I learned to like Billy Lee. I thought I should dislike him because of his occupation, but the more time we spent together the more I enjoyed his company. Liking him and accepting him didn't change my values, though.

"Why don't you go straight?" I asked him. "You could be a success at anything. You don't have to deal drugs. Besides, there's a lot of responsibility that goes along with this. People die from this stuff, Billy Lee. It makes people crazy."

Billy was intelligent. I didn't know it at the time, but he had a master's degree in business administration and a bachelor's degree in accounting. He spoke crisply and articulated his rationalizations well.

"My stuff is always clean," he insisted. "I have a lab, a chemist, the works. I take it very seriously. Nobody buys dirty drugs from me."

"That's a cop-out. If you guys didn't sell it, nobody could use it."

"That's a bunch of middle class naive jive," he responded. "That's not the problem. Dealers aren't the problem. Some of them may be rough. And some of them hurt people. But if there wasn't customer demand, there'd be no supply. Look at prohibition. They tried to get rid of the supply side and it didn't work. Consumers demanded alcohol and they got it. People like me suddenly became respectable. That's what I want to do. I'm going to get into politics and make drugs respectable."

"Billy Lee," I pleaded. "You see it from your side. I see it from the other. I have to look at your damages every day. Same way with drinking. I have to see all the mistakes. I don't give a darn about supply and demand."

"Cars kill people," he interrupted. "You don't try to get rid of car salesmen. Guns kill people; you aren't putting gun dealers in jail. I'm careful about my business. I've got my own quality control program. Nobody who works for me sells to kids. Why should we? We have an exclusive clientele—lawyers, doctors, executives. If they didn't have me to buy from they'd run the risk of getting some bad stuff and dying or something.

"I'm not the problem, John. You're missing the mark. If you want to solve the drug problem, you're going the wrong direction. As long as there's somebody looking for an easy fix, dealers will be around to sell it to them. Reduce the demand. It's as simple and complex as that."

> *Yeah, yeah. It's a bandwagon kind of thing now. But what the heck? Trends come and go, you know, like the loop things on the shirts. Drugs is a way of life, man.*
> — *Darrell (age 32) Spokane*

Why Is Drug Awareness at an All-time High?

The current drug epidemic actually began over twenty years ago, in the early 1960s, when widespread drug abuse became a part of American society. By mid-1980 people no longer had to read sterile and ponderous research studies to see the result of drug addiction. The results were across the street, next door, or in the next room. Caution that began in the early 1980s turned to alarm by 1986. Public concern reached a peak.

This alarm was heightened by the tragic deaths of athletes Len Bias on June 19, 1986, and Don Rogers one week later. The death of Bias, in particular, received wide exposure and had a major impact on Washington, D.C. society, which considers Maryland a "home team." In spite of the revelations, police reports indicated crack traffic increased immediately following Bias's death. The nation had only begun to recognize the devastating effect of crack.

Equally important, cocaine addiction started to penetrate a higher level of society. As the damage of drug abuse spread to these more politically influential levels, public outcry grew more intense, and interest in Nancy Reagan's "Just Say NO" anti-drug campaign, which was already five years old at the time, revived.

A final factor causing the issue to rise to public attention was election-year activity. No one dared challenge something as emotional and controversial as drug-abuse legislation in an election year. No one even dared to postpone recommendations until a study could determine what action to take; the press or a political opponent might interpret such inaction as "foot dragging."

In many ways attention given drug abuse in 1986 exceeded the attention given "demon rum and king liquor" during the pre-prohibition 1900s. The pre-election attention given drug abuse was phenomenal. Newspaper headlines, television specials, and even magazine covers decried the problems of crack and cocaine. In a matter of weeks, Congress wrote and passed anti-drug legislation to the figure of $1.7 billion. Campaigns for public office were stumped on the "anti-drug" theme, getting popular public response and no opposition. The focus continued intensely as anti-drug efforts soared.

Even with increased media attention and stepped-up anti-drug programs, however, addiction is increasing. The use of tobacco is increasing. The use of tranquilizers and other prescription drugs is increasing. The use of cocaine and crack is increasing. And recent statistics indicate that the rate of alcoholism is rising, especially among adolescents. Only the use of heroin and some other hard drugs has remained stable.

Increased anti-drug efforts by the media and government are commendable, but they are not enough. If all the media does is sandwich anti-drug public service announcements between programs that model drug-using behavior and advertisements that advocate the use of alcohol and over-the-counter drugs, we cannot expect the announcements to have much positive effect. And if all government does is support anti-drug legislation, but continues to subsidize the tobacco industry, we shouldn't be surprised if we see few positive results. In these cases, actions do indeed speak louder than words. As long as we continue to send mixed signals to our children, we can expect them to be confused.

We've already established the cause of the problem: Our

children are growing up in a culture that believes a quick cure is a proper cure, that considers "drive-through meals" a standard of excellence, that spells relief a-n-t-a-c-i-d, and that believes "If it's time to relax, it's time for a beer."

We've also established what the answer *is not*: Protecting our children from drugs is impossible, and protecting them from the consequences of drug use is unwise. One teacher, disgusted after intercepting drugs being purchased on her elementary school playground, put it this way: "If we held school on the moon, dealers would build their own space shuttle to get there." So protection is not the issue. Giving our children a chance is the issue.

> *I don't think it's fair for them to expect us to give up anything. Just because our drugs are illegal and their drugs aren't. That really shouldn't matter.*
> — *Bonnie (age 16) Oakland*

"So what do you think the problem is?" asked a man in the back row. "All the statistics back up what you say, but what do you think is the reason? It would seem to me that folks would get it together and stamp this thing out."

I was speaking to the faculty of a college preparatory school that was having problems with student drug use. The question came from a large, totally bald man who looked more like a professional wrestler than an artist, which I learned later he was.

"It would seem that way to me too. But we don't. It's as simple as that."

"But why?" he interrupted. "Why do you think that's true?"

"I honestly am puzzled about it," I began. "What is your teaching field again?" I asked.

"Music," he responded. "Mainly piano." I thought about this man's huge hands moving over a delicate piano keyboard. It seemed oddly incongruent.

"Music, right. Well, I'll give you my opinion, but it's a lot like music and other art forms. If you write a piece of music it's neither right nor wrong. It's music, right? Well, that's what my opinion is like."

"Fine," he laughed. "Just don't play off-key, okay?"

"I'll try not to," I grinned. "I really don't want to answer this because I might alienate some of you and I've got some important things to say before I leave. But I'll risk it. Mind you, this is only my opinion and I have little to base it on except my beliefs and experience.

"I think our society is basically an honest one. I think Americans are generally straightforward and don't tolerate hypocrisy very well. And that's the core of the problem. If we want to solve the problem of *juvenile* drug abuse we've got to start with the problems adults have. And we're not ready to do that. The studies I talked about earlier all indicate this is a societal problem. If you use tranquilizers, your child will use drugs. If you drink, your child will. If you use over-the-counter drugs, your children will likely use 'under-the-counter' drugs. If you smoke tobacco, your children are likely to smoke marijuana. There are a lot of implications there.

"Sure, I'm exaggerating to make the point, but evidence shows there's truth in what I'm saying. But the saddest part of it is that we're not ready to give up all that. If we're going to get serious about the drug addiction problem in this country, though, that's where we have to look. To do anything else would be a waste of time. If we want to raise non-drug-seeking children we have to raise them in a non-drug-seeking society, which we don't have.

"If Americans start focusing intensely on the drug problem, they begin to feel hypocritical. Rather than be hypocrites, they let it go, I think. It's sort of like an unconscious deal. You don't say anything about my drinking and I won't say anything about your marijuana."

"You smoke?" the music teacher asked.

"No." I shook my head.

"Drink?"

"Nope."

"So what's your drug?" he searched.

"I don't know. I'm a diet soda freak. Maybe it's caffeine. But I'll tell you what, I'm part of the problem. We're all part of it. And until we pull together to do something about it, we'll all suffer together."

> It doesn't matter. You can make just about anything in a lab any more. They take all the coke off the street, it doesn't matter. You can get synthetics and make an analog. It's easy.
> — Willard (age 19) Washington

What Are the Trends in Drug Abuse?

The "war on drugs" has been raging for several generations, but drugs are winning and those fighting have suffered massive casualties.

One alarming trend is the use and manufacture of synthetic drugs. One of the problems with synthetic drugs is that new ones are so easy to make they can't be outlawed quickly enough. MDMA (better known as ecstasy) was sold legally on college campuses as recently as 1984. As soon as it was outlawed other legal synthetics appeared, such as Eve and Rhapsody. Recent experiments conducted on animals dramatically illustrate the power of these drugs. Monkeys offered a choice of synthetic cocaine or food will consistently take the synthetic drug, even to the point of starvation. Other experiments have illustrated that a genetic predisposition to use dangerous drugs can be bred into laboratory animals.

Drug enforcement agents have noticed other alarming trends. Computers are being used to design combinations of narcotics and other drugs, which appear almost weekly. Cocoa paste, the crude extract of the coca leaf and more potent than crack, is also becoming widely used. If its availability increases in this country the effects could be more deadly than those of the popular crack.

Current statistics indicate that fewer than 30 percent of

cocaine addicts who are treated professionally will succeed in their first attempt at rehabilitation. For heroin addicts the odds are bleaker. The success rate for first-time addicts is 2 percent. The approach to treatment is described by many experts as simply "too naive." As an example, addicts often drop out of drug-treatment programs after three or four weeks of hospitalization, just long enough to flush the drugs from their systems. In most cases, their reason for leaving is not due to a false sense of confidence. The reason more often is that four weeks is usually the maximum coverage allowed by health insurance plans. By limiting coverage in this way, health insurance companies become part of the addiction problem. Unintentionally, they define the problem as minor and become part of the system of denial in which most addicts live. This denial was illustrated dramatically by Sam, who entered a rehabilitation center for alcoholism treatment.

"What's an alcoholic anyway?" Sam asked defiantly. "Isn't it a person whose drinking is out of control?"

I studied him in the chair across from me. He was the picture of a successful salesman. And that's precisely what he was. In fact, he was vice president of sales for a large company. A crisply starched shirt fit snugly under his gray woolen suit. Black wing tip shoes and a maroon tie highlighted his "dress for success" look. His business life was a success. But his personal and family life was a failure.

"No, I'm serious," he said. "How do you decide if somebody's an alcoholic? Do you give them a test or what? I want to take it. Let's go."

"Sam," I responded, "you told me you're drinking every night till bedtime. A six-pack or so, right? Then you go to sleep wherever you happen to be at the moment. When you get up the next morning you go to the office. Same thing starts at seven or so when you get home that night. And this goes on five nights a week?"

"Right," he answered quickly. "But I only drink when I'm around my wife. So what's the problem? If she's not there, I don't drink. I don't see there's a drinking problem. Seems to me I have a wife problem. If you get her straightened out I'll be okay. Deal?" He smiled. "How about it?"

"You sound like a salesman to me." Sam was at his persuasive best. And I had heard it all before. The denial of any responsibility is one of the primary symptoms of addiction. Most of it is usually very convincing.

"Look, John, the drinking is not a problem. I don't drink because I'm out of control. I drink because I want to. I want to escape all the pressure of my marriage. But I *decide* to do that. So it's not like I'm some sort of alcoholic or something."

"And what do you say about the DUI's?" I asked, referring to his three arrests for driving under the influence. One had been dismissed. On another he was acquitted. But the third time he was convicted, which led to our counseling session. Sam would not agree to enter inpatient or outpatient treatment, but he did agree to counseling. I agreed to see him three times, with the understanding he would terminate at that point if I believed there was an addiction problem. If he had a drinking problem and I saw him for marriage or family counseling I would become a conspirator in the advancement of his disease. I did not want to become a part of his denial. I could unintentionally make the problem worse. Sam was aware of all this and also aware that I would recommend inpatient treatment to his employer if I found it appropriate. I would never discuss what he said in my sessions, but my understanding with Sam and his employer was that I would make a recommendation after three visits.

"You admit you've been drinking since you were a teenager. You didn't even know your wife then. Blaming her is a cop-out."

"John," he grunted. "Anybody can get a ticket. You could get one." He ignored the second part of my comment.

"And I have," I agreed. "But not for DUI. That's something I don't do."

"Come on." He smiled. "You know how it is. Listen. I swear. Make my wife better and I won't drink." He raised his right hand in the air as if taking an oath. "I swear. That drinking when I was a kid was just playing around, you know?"

I shook my head. "Sam, you are one of the most persuasive and likeable human beings I have ever met. I'd like to be able to help you. So show me something. Go one week without drinking. I'm supposed to see you one more time, a week from tonight. Show me."

"If I do that," he asked, "will you recommend to Glenn that I don't have to go through inpatient treatment? Will you tell him I can work with you?"

"Tell you what," I said. "If you can do that and your wife tells me you made it, that'll go a long way. The way it sounds right now, though, you have a major drinking problem. I think you probably suffer from long-term alcoholism. So you've got some persuading to do. But making it for a week would help."

"Doctor," he stood up and stuck out his hand, "you drive a hard bargain. But I accept your challenge. Empty beer mugs at thirty paces. Bring your second and I'll meet you at sunrise. I'll be sober as a judge all week long. It's a deal."

I rose from my seat and shook his outstretched hand. "Deal!" I agreed. "And give me two dollar's worth of whatever you're selling!" I chuckled as he left. I wanted to see him make it, but I had seen so many others fail. . . .

Forty-eight hours later I received a telephone call from Sam's wife. He had been arrested for driving while intoxicated that very day.

> *People are suspicious of you if you don't use something. They think you're a narc or somebody boring. It's a good way not to be liked.*
> *— Carrie (age 15) Manchester*

What Are the Trends in Drug Prevention?

We've already established that drug abuse is a family problem, and if the core cultural value of our society is to change we must begin with this basic unit. If enough families respond, the drug-abuse problem will be history. Parents can begin that change today. School teachers can. Youth directors can. Children can even begin that sort of change with each other.

Perhaps the change has already begun. Police officers are working with children in Los Angeles schools by helping the children build self-esteem. They help them practice saying "no." In July 1986 Nancy Reagan met with the Reverend Jesse Jackson to discuss the drug problem. They agreed drug abuse "crosses all party, color, and economic lines." It's a society problem, they suggested, and all society must join hands to defeat it.

That is happening in some cases. A Chicago-based electric utility, Commonwealth Edison, started an anti-drug program in 1982. They offered treatment to those needing help and screened new employees more thoroughly. Since the treatment and prevention efforts started, absenteeism has decreased 25 percent, medical claims are down 17 percent, and on-the-job accidents have decreased significantly. A recent government report on civil service employees found treatment programs pay for themselves through reduced medical costs within two years. Similar results are discovered frequently by other corporations.

In the United States, many of those arrested for driving while intoxicated are forced to attend educational and treatment programs. The same is true in some communities for those arrested for public drunkenness. The British have a similar treatment for those on harder drugs. A maintenance supply of drugs is provided to allow detoxification to occur safely. The user must register with the government as an addict and participate in rehabilitation efforts. The approach seems to be working well. The per capita addiction rate is far less in Britain. The illicit drug market is also smaller and far less lucrative. British addicts have a reduced need for excessive money to purchase their drugs illicitly, so the crime rate has diminished. Similar programs are being considered on an experimental basis in the United States, but have not been popularly supported.

The remedies for the problem are as complex as the causes.

It has taken well over 300 years for the problem in American society to reach its current level. A "quick fix" cure is unlikely. The cost of treating those already addicted as well as the cost of reversing current trends will be steep, both financially and socially. But such costs are far less than the cost of allowing the problem to continue at its current rate of growth.

In a message to the major television networks, 300 legislators asked for help. They sought "an unprecedented, coordinated offensive against the culture that encourages the use of cocaine, crack, and other dangerous drugs." It is this kind of major cooperative venture that is required. Drugs and their power will not be eradicated by any one law. Neither will they be eradicated by the death of another athlete. It will take diligence and patience.

Unfortunately, however, diligence and patience are not known as the great American virtues. As Texas Congressman Jim Wright says, "One of the vast unfortunate by-products of the television age is the short attention span of the American public. We walk along . . . happy until a crisis grabs us. . . . Once it is off . . . nightly television coverage, we go back to sleep."

We cannot risk going back to sleep. If we do, we all lose. Not just congressmen, not just children, not just families. We all lose. We cannot allow it to happen.

I eventually lost contact with Billy Lee Thompson. I wondered if he had ever gotten into politics. While working on this manuscript I attempted to contact him several times. One person mentioned he had heard that Billy Lee had moved to Arizona to attend law school. That seems as likely as anything.

I believe Billy Lee's peculiar brand of wisdom can be helpful. Maybe he was right. Perhaps we should shift our focus off the drug dealer, about whom we can do little, and onto ourselves and our children. If we can teach our children to live without drugs, eventually the demand for his product will diminish. And when the demand dries up, Billy Lee and his colleagues will find some other way to make a living. But the demand is still there. It's everywhere. And as long as it exists Billy Lee Thompson and thousands like him will prey upon our children.

Regardless of how much we abhor Billy Lee's profession, we must thank him for one thing—he has told us how to help our children. But the real question remains, "What will we do tomorrow?"

Questions for Inquiry

1. Investigations into the cause of the space shuttle accident that ended seven lives will result in safer space travel for astronauts. What might happen if similar mass intensity, scrutiny, and action were applied to the drug problem?
2. If your child is using drugs, use the four following suggestions to find out what he or she is looking for or trying to escape from:
   a. Listen more carefully and with acceptance.
   b. Disclose your own human frailties.
   c. Spend time getting to know your child's friends.
   d. Make yourself available to your child when he or she needs you instead of when it is convenient for you.
3. What action(s) suggested in the Epilogue will you pursue in an effort to provide a more drug-free environment? As a family? As a church member? As an individual member of society?

Family or Group Activity

Discuss the faulty core value of our society concerning drug use. Consider how, on the one hand, we encourage drug use (to get relief, to feel good, to feel "in," etc.) and yet we fail to support people who get in trouble or become addicted. Solicit your children's thoughts about the problem as well as their ideas as to what needs to be done about it.

Journal Entry

Having finished reading this book, decide whether or not to continue your drug-free behavior. Record your prediction as to how this decision will affect your life, and your children's lives, a year from now, five years from now, etc.

For Further Thought

Consider that for twenty years we have had warning labels on cigarettes. During that time, tobacco use increased. In light of this apparent lack of regard to health-hazard warnings, how effective do you think our fight against drug use will be if it focuses on fear tactics? After reading the Epilogue, determine what actions you think *would* be effective.

EPILOGUE

On March 11, 1987, I was guest speaker at a meeting of child-care workers from throughout the southeastern United States. I had been asked to address the general topic of adolescent stress and to comment specifically on the teenage suicide phenomenon. During a scheduled break I was approached by two television crews wanting an interview. Rarely does a conference such as this attract the attention of the news media, so I was surprised at their attention.

"What's the big deal?" I asked. "Slow news day, or what?"

"Haven't you heard?" one stern-faced reporter asked. "Four teenagers killed themselves last night in a suicide pact. They were discovered this morning."

I shuddered at my attempt at humor. "I'm sorry," I sighed. "What can I do to help?"

Within the following week at least six more children in our country committed suicide. National attention once again focused on the tremendous stress placed on adolescents today. On March 18, a week after the New Jersey suicides, I was again speaking on adolescent stress, this time at a large church. The first person to meet me was a man who appeared to be in his early thirties.

"Hi," he called out. "I saw you at 4:15 this morning on CNN. And now here you are!"

"What in the world were you doing up at 4:00 A.M.?" I questioned.

"Trying to get my two year old to bed," he laughed. "Maybe she heard you were going to be on television." We joked for a few minutes about two year olds and then it was time for me to begin my presentation. I spoke for forty-five minutes and then asked for questions. The first person to raise her hand was the mother of a teenage girl.

"You have talked a lot about the problems families have to face. But what is something concrete we can do? If we really care, what do you recommend?"

"That's a complex question, but a very good one. First, I want to point out that all of this is connected. Stress, drug abuse, and suicide are all part of the same problem and symptomatic of the same poisoning going on in society. You can respond on several levels. On the family level I suggest practicing the "ABC's" I mentioned earlier. This is especially true of spending time with your children. They need time, especially during such crises as we are facing now. If you're not sure how to do these things, we can discuss it more later.

"On the local church level, apparently most of you are already doing something. The fact that you're here means you're concerned. But involvement is the key. The Boy Scout leader in here earlier demonstrated that. Did you see what he was doing? One family just moved here from Texas. Moving is stressful for teenagers. So here is your Boy Scout leader trying to recruit their thirteen year old into the group. That's great. We need more of that kind of involvement with teenagers. What he's doing might save that young man's life. I think the church is missing a great opportunity to help some teenagers. The more adult involvement you give these teenagers, the more likely they are to be stress-free. Churches are also a great platform for discussion groups and general rap sessions about drug abuse and other problems children face. It is a safe place for serious, deep-level education and prevention programs.

"On the society level there's a lot you can do. I guarantee, radio, television, all media respond to letters from viewers. I've forgotten the exact number, but they assume that one letter represents the opinions of several hundred people who didn't write. If everyone in this room wrote a letter each time a commercial aired that advocated drug or alcohol use, the commercials would soon disappear. Your government leaders also pay attention to mail. This is especially true of elected officials. If you have deep convictions about all of this, write letters to the media, government officials, even your insurance company. What does your insurance policy say about coverage for alcohol or drug problems? Find out. If they don't cover it, get different insurance. That will get their attention.

"There's a lot you can do. Doing something that might fail is not a mistake; doing nothing at all is the mistake. These problems will change only when we make them change. It's action that's important. . . ."

Three days after I spoke at the church an Associated Press headline announced: "Autopsies find cocaine and alcohol in 4 teens." The report went on to describe the three nineteen year olds and one seventeen year old who had died earlier in the suicide pact. All had significant levels of both cocaine and alcohol in their bloodstreams at the time of their deaths. Larry McClure, Bergen County, New Jersey prosecutor, described the four as being "on the downside of the cocaine they used."

Death is the downside. If life and health are the question, drugs are not the answer. Perhaps part of the answer came at 11:00 P.M. that same night when the phone rang unexpectedly.

"Hey, big guy. I just saw you on TV! How's it going?" It was the familiar voice of my friend John Shaheen, the president of World Carpets in nearby Dalton, Georgia.

"Oh, hi John," I responded. "Thanks for calling. So I was on TV tonight?"

"Yeah," he responded. "You did good. Obviously it wasn't live."

"Nope," I answered. "Not this time."

"Listen, I didn't call just to flatter you. I want to make an offer you can't refuse."

"Okay," I laughed. "Shoot!"

"I don't know whether or not you have any contacts up in

New Jersey, but if you can get someone up there to let you help get those problems worked out, we'll pick up your expenses— plane fare, everything. World Carpets will support you."

I was astounded. "That's great, John. That is so generous. I can't believe you guys would do something like that. Thank you."

"Well," he sighed. "I'm just really scared. I don't want those kids to kill themselves. And I think you can help them. I remember what it was like when I was a teenager. I used to get pretty lonely and burned out myself. I just think we owe it to kids to help if we can. . . ."

John Shaheen of World Carpets inspired me. When all of corporate America reaches out the way he has, I believe the drug problem will disappear. The answer is in front of us. It is caring, an action verb. Love in action.

"It's the least we can do," John added. "Christ reached out to those in need. We need to do the same. So let's do it!"

APPENDIX A—
DRUG AWARENESS CHART

Name/Average Cost	Street Name	Method of Consumption	Experiences	Signs and Symptoms of Use	Consequences of Use
ALCOHOL Whiskey, gin, beer, wine, *orange juice & vodka	PGA—Pure grain Booze	Drink	Intoxication, unsteady gait, slurred speech, relaxed inhibitions, impaired coordination, slowed reflexes	Smell of alcohol on clothes or breath, hangover, glazed eyes, intoxicated behavior *No smell of alcohol	Addiction, overdose—when mixed with other depressants, accidents due to impaired judgment/ability, heart/liver damage
NICOTINE Cigarettes, cigars, chewing tobacco, snuff.		Smoke, chew, or snort	Stimulation, relaxation	Coughing, yellow stains on hands, burnt holes in clothing, matches, cigarette butts, cellophane	Lung cancer, chronic cough, diseases of blood/heart vessels—addiction
CANNABIS Marijuana ($150/oz.) Hashish ($300/oz.)	Joint, grass, pot, toke, reefer, roach, weed, dope, Acapulco gold, jive, Texas tea, shit, Taiwan stick, hemp, hash, bhang	Smoke or chew	Poor coordination, decreased concentration, dry mouth, hunger, involuntary laughing, euphoria, hallucinations	Rolling papers, pipes, dried plant material, roach clips, odor of burnt hemp rope, red eyes, incoordination, inappropriate laughter	Addiction, impaired short-term memory, panic reaction, depression or anxiety
DEPRESSANTS Barbiturates Nembutal Seconal ($3-5/pill) Veronal Doriden Chloralhydrate Tranquilizers Valium Miltown Librium Thorazine Stelazine	Downers, candy, barbs, goof balls, dolls, yellow jackets, red, blue heavens, purple hearts, peanuts, pink, red devils, rainbows, greenie	Swallow	Drowsiness, slurred speech, short attention span, intoxication, reduced or labored breathing, slowed heart beat	Capsules, pills, inappropriate behavior, combativeness, violence, excessive sleeping, pinpoint pupils	Addiction, overdose, especially when used with alcohol, muscle rigidity
Quaaludes ($4-6/pill)	Ludes, 714's		Mild hallucinations, moodiness, relaxation, dry mouth	Detached appearance, loss of contact with reality	

Name/Average Cost	Street Name	Method of Consumption	Experiences	Signs and Symptoms of Use	Consequences of Use
STIMULANTS Amphetamines Benzedrine ($3-5/dose) Methedrine Dexedrine Methamphetamine ($80/gram) Diet pills Caffeine Phenolprop Anolamine PPA	Uppers, speed, black beauties, bennies, happy pills, meth, bam, dexies, jolly beans, roses, peaches, oranges, cartwheels, fake speed, boots, bootleg	Swallow or inject	Dry mouth, dry nose, nervousness, bad breath	Chapped, dry lips, dilated pupils, excessive sleeplessness, noticeable rubbing/scratching of nose, appetite loss, bad breath	Hepatitis, injection-site infection, AIDS, endocarditis, psychosis, brain damage, death
Cocaine ($25/dose, 20% pure), Crack ($5/dose, 90% pure)	Coke, snow, gold dust, dust, star dust, Bernice, flake, Corine, speedball— with heroin	Sniff, inject, or smoke	Intensely brief euphoria, exceptional feeling of well-being followed by depression, increased heart rate and blood pressure, restlessness, rush of excitement	Glass vials, glass, syringes, white crystalline powder, razor blades, pipes, needle marks or scars	AIDS, addiction, heart attack, seizures, lung damage, paranoia, marked depression, death
HALLUCINOGENS LSD ($3-5/dose) PCP ($3-5/dose) Mescaline ($3-5/dose) Peyote	Acid, trip Angel dust Mushrooms	Swallow, inject, or chew	Altered perceptions and mood, panic, anxiety. Inappropriate focus on details, nausea, confused sensations, disorientation, hyperthermia, piloerection	Tablets, capsules, micordots, blotter squares, odor on breath or clothing, dilated pupils, animated or bizzare behavior	Violent and unpredictable behavior, emotional instability, flashbacks (recurrences of experiences after immediate effects of drugs wear off), AIDS

Name/Average Cost	Street Name	Method of Consumption	Experiences	Signs and Symptoms of Use	Consequences of Use
DESIGNER DRUGS DMT MDMA ($25/dose) STP	Big D Ecstacy, love drug Adam	Swallow, inject, or chew	Similar to hallucinogens. See book for discussion.	See book for discussion	See book for discussion
INHALANTS Glue Gasoline Aerosols White Out Amylnitrite Antihistimine Nutmeg	Huff, gas, glue, gold paint	Inhale	Uncoordination, confusion, reduced control, dizziness, headaches, drowsiness	Empty glue/solvent containers, plastic bags, odor of substance on clothing and breath, appearance of intoxication, red watery eyes, poor coordination, vomiting	Unconsciousness, asphyxiation—from plastic bag used to inhale fumes, hepatitis, renal injury, disorientation, brain damage, sudden death
HALLUCINOGEN/ DEPRESSANT Talwin ($8/dose) Pyrobenzamine ($25/dose)	T's & B's, T's and Blues, Teddies & Betties, T-shirts & Blue jeans	Inject	Rush of euphoria, lethargy, constipation	Bent spoons, cotton (for filtering), phone callers selling t-shirts/blue jeans, constricted pupils, needle marks	Infection from contaminated syringes, AIDS, death from overdose
ANTIDEPRESSANTS Elavil Tricyclics Tofranil Siniquan Nardil Parnate Ritalin		Swallow	Depression lifted, drowsiness, stimulation, mouth dryness, blurred vision, skin rash	Pills, tablets	Jaundice, tremor, overdose, death

Name/Average Cost	Street Name	Method of Consumption	Experiences	Signs and Symptoms of Use	Consequences of Use
NARCOTICS Opium Heroin Morphine ($3/pill) Codeine ($10/dose) (Tylenol #3 & #4) Methadone Percodan ($3/dose) Demoral ($3/dose) Dilaudid ($40-65/dose) Mexican heroin	Dope (brown) Junk H, skag, smack M, dreamer, Miss, Emma Jones Scat Joy powder Black tar Tar, tootsie roll, gumbo	Inject, smoke, or swallow	Insensitivity to pain, nausea, vomiting, euphoria, lethargy, drowsiness, watery eyes, runny nose, constipation	Syringes, swabs, bent spoons, pinpoint pupils, red nose, white power around nostrils, medicinal breath, cold, moist skin, inappropriate clothing (i.e. long sleeves to cover needle marks or scars on arms)	AIDS, addiction, disorientation, significant weight loss, hepatitis, overdose, contamination from unsterile needles

APPENDIX B—GLOSSARY

Acapulco Gold: A high grade of marijuana.

Angel Dust: Mixture of marijuana and PCP.

Antabuse: Given to alcoholics to discourage drinking. Ingestion of alcohol after taking this drug causes nausea and vomiting.

Bag: A container of drugs.

Bang: To inject drugs.

Bennies: Benzedrine or amphetamine capsules.

Big John: The police, the heat, the fuzz.

Blanks: Diluted narcotics.

Blast: A strong effect from a drug.

Brick: A kilogram of marijuana.

Burned: Cheated in a drug transaction.

Cap: A capsule of powdered drugs.

Chipping, Chippying: Occasional use of drugs.

Clean: Having no possession of drugs when arrested.

Cold Turkey: Sudden withdrawal from drug use.

Come down: Recovering from a drug high.

Cop: To acquire heroin.

Crash: To come down hard from a drug high. Also, to spend the night, e.g., "Where can we crash for the night?"

Crystal: Speed

Cut: To adulterate or alter a drug.

Designers: A new category of synthetic drugs—very powerful.

Dime bag: A ten-dollar purchase of drugs.

Dolls: Barbiturates and amphetamines.

Downer: A depressant such as a barbiturate.

Drop: To swallow a drug, e.g., "to drop acid."

Fix: A drug injection, usually heroin; a "hit."

Flip out: To have a bad drug "trip."

Freak: Amphetamine user.

Grass: Marijuana.

H: Heroin.

Hallucinogenic: Psychoactive, psychomimetic, psychedelic.

Hard stuff: Morphine, heroin, cocaine.

Hash: Hashish.

Head: Marijuana user.

High: A feeling of exhilaration or well-being produced by a drug.

Hit: A single quantity of a drug sufficient to create a high or altered state of consciousness; also means to inject a drug into a vein successfully.

Inebriated: As from alcohol: Plastered, high, drunk, loaded, stewed.

Joint: A marijuana cigarette.

Junkie: Narcotics addict.

Lid: An ounce of marijuana.

LSD: Acid, trip, cubes, sugar cubes, big D.

Mainline: To inject drugs intravenously, also pop, fix, bang, shoot, hit.

Narc: Originally, a narcotics detective or agent: Big John, the Bull, Sam, Whiskers; now used to refer to anyone suspected of turning in drug abusers.

Nickle bag: A five-dollar bag of drugs.

O.D.: Overdose.

Pop: To inject drugs under the skin; to swallow pills.

Pot: Marijuana.

Pusher: One who sells drugs, also called a dealer.

Red devil: A seconal capsule; also called reds.

Reefer: Marijuana cigarette.

Roach: The last part of a marijuana cigarette that is smoked.

Ropes: Veins.

Run: The use of speed for several days nonstop without coming down from a high.

Rush: The rapid onset of feeling good after an intravenous injection.

Scag: Heroin.

Score: To buy drugs, as in "I scored a high."

Shoot: To inject drugs.

Smack: Heroin.

Snort: To inhale drugs, such as cocaine.

Spaced out: A state of being high or of altered consciousness—not necessarily from drugs.

Speedballs: Powerful mixture of heroin and cocaine.

Spike: A syringe or hypodermic needle.

Stash: The supply of drugs on hand.

Stoned: High on drugs—usually marijuana; high, turned on, ripped.

Straight: Square, doesn't use drugs.

Strung out: To be ill from drug withdrawal.

Stuff: Drugs.

T's & B's or T's & Blues: Talwin and pyrobenzamine, taken together to get high. Also called teddies and betties, teddas and bettas, t-shirts and blue jeans.

Toke up: Smoke marijuana.

Tracks: Marks or scars left by hypodermic needles resulting from repeated intravenous injections.

Trip: Experience following ingestion of a hallucinogenic drug.

Upper: A stimulant such as amphetamines.

Weed: Marijuana.

Works: Equipment for mainlining, also called artillery, includes a hypodermic needle (spike), a match (burner), a spoon or cap (cooker), and a cotton strainer.

Yellow jacket: Nembutal capsules.

Zonked: Extremely intoxicated by a drug. Unnerved by an experience.

APPENDIX C—QUESTIONNAIRE

Directions: Answer the questions below with one child in mind. Each question is supported by various research studies or significant clinical evidence. The references to gender (he or she) are used only for descriptive purposes and are not intended to limit the question to one sex. Answer each question as accurately as possible. Circle your response and add the total points after completing the questionnaire. Compare the final score with those at the end of the questionnaire.

1. *Do the child's parents drink or use other psychoactive drugs?*   Never = 0   Occasionally = 2   Often = 3

2. *Does the child associate with peers who are known to drink or use drugs regularly?*
                          Never = 0   Occasionally = 2   Often = 3

3. *Do parents and peers both drink or use drugs regularly?*
                          No = 0   Yes = 2

4. *Does the child's mother use tranquilizers?*
                          Never = 0   Occasionally = 2   Often = 3

5. *Does the child smoke cigarettes?*
                          No = 0   Yes = 2

6. *Do the parents regularly use over-the-counter drugs?*
                          No = 0   Seldom = 2   Often = 3

7. *Do the parents smoke cigarettes?*
                          No = 0   Yes = 2

8. *Is there a history of alcoholism or other drug addiction in the family?*   No = 0   Yes = 2

9. *Does the child seem to know the difference between right and wrong and have a healthy conscience?*

Yes = 0   No = 2

10. *Do the child's parents spend time in one-on-one interaction with the child?*   Often = 0   Seldom = 2

11. *Does the child complain of boredom?*

Rarely = 0   Often = 2

12. *Are family rules, structure, and guidelines articulated and written down for the child?*   Yes = 0   No = 1

13. *Could the child's father (or male role model) be described as hypermasculine?*   No = 0   Yes = 1

14. *Is the child male?*

No = 0   Yes = 1

15. *Is the child punished by excessive spanking or other harsh measures?*

Never = 0   Occasionally = 1   Often = 2

16. *Is the child allowed to experience the natural consequences of his/her choices? Is discipline enforced in the home by non-corporal measures?*   Yes = 0   No = 1

17. *Have drugs, drug paraphernalia, or drug culture evidence been found on the child's person, room, or clothes?*

No = 0   Yes = 3

18. *Have the child's family or friends complained of money or personal property missing from home?*

No = 0   Yes = 1

19. *Does the child appear withdrawn or alienated?*

No = 0   Occasionally = 1   Often = 2

20. *Does the child participate in activities supervised by adults such as clubs, athletic teams, or youth groups?*

Often = 0   Occasionally = 1   No = 2

21. *Does the child have significant adult relationships other than parents?*   Yes = 0   No = 2

22. *Has the child been caught telling lies regularly?*

No = 0   Yes = 1

23. *Does the child attend church?*

Often = 0   Seldom = 1   Never = 2

24. *Does the child practice self-discipline in areas such as*

studying, homework, or chores?

Often = 0 Occasionally = 1 Never = 2

25. Do authority figures in the child's life (parents, teachers, youth leaders, etc.) use fear and guilt as a way of controlling the child's behavior?

Never = 0 Occasionally = 1 Often = 2

26. Does the child appear to think and make decisions impulsively? No = 0 Yes = 1

27. Was the child ever diagnosed as hypertensive or hyperkinetic? No = 0 Yes = 2

28. Does the child ever exhibit any of the signs or symptoms of depression listed elsewhere in this book?

Never = 0 Occasionally = 2 Often = 3

29. Has the child been observed with dilated or pin-pointed pupils, eye redness, unusual nose rubbing, or persistent coughing? Never = 0 Occasionally = 2 Often = 3

30. Has the child's speech pattern been slurred or inappropriate? Never = 0 Occasionally = 1

31. Has the child exhibited any violent, unpredictable, or bizarre behavior?

Never = 0 Occasionally = 2 Often = 3

32. Have you observed any poorly coordinated movements such as stumbling or running into objects?

Never = 0 Occasionally = 1

33. Does the child respond favorably if asked whether he likes himself? Yes = 0 No = 2

34. Does the child refer to herself in negative terms such as "slob," "dummy," "nerd," etc.?

No = 0 Occasionally = 2 Often = 3

35. Is the child an only child?

No = 0 Yes = 3

36. Does the child live in a single-parent home?

No = 0 Yes = 3

37. Does the child have frequent fights and stand-offs with friends? No = 0 Occasionally = 2 Often = 3

38. Is the child in frequent trouble at school, with legal authorities, or other adults?

No = 0 Occasionally = 2 Often = 3

39. *Do adults typically solve problems for the child?*
                No = 0   Occasionally = 2   Often = 3
40. *If the child lives in a single-parent home, how often does he see the non-custodial parent?*
                Often = 0   Occasionally = 1   Never = 3
41. *Is the child exposed to excessive family conflict?*
                Never = 0   Occasionally = 1   Often = 2
42. *Has the child experienced any of the following stressful events in the past two years: death of a family member; death of a friend; divorce of parents; moving; lengthy illness (such as mononucleosis)?*   No = 0   Yes = 2 (for each event)

Add up your total points. The closer you come to 100 the higher potential for drug use, i.e.: 50 points = 50 percent chance; 80 = 80 percent chance.

APPENDIX D—TWELVE STEPS
ALCOHOLICS ANONYMOUS

1. We admitted we were powerless over alcohol—that our lives had become unmanageable.
2. We came to believe that a Power greater than ourselves could restore us to sanity.
3. We made a decision to turn our will and our lives over to the care of God *as we understood Him.*
4. We made a searching and fearless moral inventory of ourselves.
5. We admitted to God, to ourselves, and to another human being the exact nature of our wrongs.
6. We were entirely ready to have God remove all these defects of character.
7. We humbly asked Him to remove our shortcomings.
8. We made a list of all persons we had harmed, and became willing to make amends to them all.
9. We made direct amends to people wherever possible, except when to do so would injure them or others.
10. We continued to take personal inventory and when we were wrong promptly admitted it.
11. We sought through prayer and meditation to improve our conscious contact with God *as we understood Him,* praying only for knowledge of His will for us and the power to carry that out.
12. Having had a spiritual awakening as the result of these

steps, we tried to carry this message to alcoholics, and to practice these principles in all our affairs.

"God grant me the serenity to accept the things I cannot change, the courage to change the things I can, and the wisdom to know the difference."

(The Twelve Steps are reprinted with permission of Alcoholics Anonymous World Services International.)

REFERENCES

Adams, Edgar, and Jack Druell. "Cocaine: A Growing Public Health Problem." National Institution of Drug Abuse Division of Epidemiology and Statistical Analysis: Research Monograph Series, 50 (1984): 9–14.

Alexander, C. N. "Alcohol and Adolescent Rebellion." Social Forces 45 (1967): 542–50.

Alexander, G. "LSD: Injections Early in Pregnancy Produce Abnormalities in Offspring of Rats." Science 157 (1967): 459–60.

Ashley, Richard. "Cocaine: Its History, Uses, and Effects." New York: St. Martin's Press, 1975.

Ashton, Casswell (Department of Community Health, University of Auckland School of Medicine). "Estimated Cost of Alcohol to the New Zealand Public Hospital System." New Zealand Medical Journal 97, no. 765 (Oct. 10, 1984): 683–86.

Becker, Howard. "Becoming a Marijuana User." American Journal of Sociology 59 (Nov. 1953): 235–42.

Beschner, G. M., and A. S. Friedman (National Institute on Drug Abuse). "Treatment of Adolescent Drug Abusers." International Journal of Addictions 220, nos. 6–7 (June/July 1985): 971–93.

Blum, R. H. Society and Drugs. Vol. 1: Society and Cultural Observations. San Francisco: Josey Bass, 1970.

Blumfield, Michael, Alberto Serrano, et al. (Community Guidance Clinic, San Antonio, Texas). "Marijuana Use in High School Students." Diseases of the Nervous System 33 (Sept. 1972): 603–10.

Carroll, Jerome, Thomas Malloy, and Fern Kenrich (Eagleville Hospital and Rehabilitation Services, Pennsylvania). "Alcohol Abuse by Drug Dependent Persons: A Literature Review & Evaluation."

American Journal of Drug and Alcohol Abuse 4, no. 3 (1977): 293–315.

Craig, Starlett, and Barry Brown (Narcotics Treatment Administration). "Comparison of Youthful Heroin Users and Non-Users From One Urban Community." *International Journal of the Addictions* 10, no. 1 (1975): 53–64.

Cusfield, Joseph. *Symbolic Crusade: Status, Politics and the American Temperance Movement.* Urbana: University of Illinois Press, 1963.

DuPont, R. L. *Marijuana and Health: Fifth Annual Report to the U.S. Congress.* Rockville, Md.: National Institute on Drug Abuse, 1975.

Egger, Garry, R. A. Webb, and Ingrid Reynolds (Health Commission of New South Wales, Sidney, Australia). "Early Adolescent Antecedents of Narcotics Abuse." *International Journal of the Addictions* 13, no. 5 (1978): 773–81.

Ellinwood, Everett H. (Duke University Medical Center). "Assault & Homicide Associated with Amphetamine Abuse." *American Journal of Psychiatry* 127, no. 9 (March 1971): 1170–75.

Fagerberg, Seigfried, and Karen Fagerberg (University of Florida). "Student Attitudes Concerning Drug Abuse Education and Prevention." *Journal of Drug Education* 6, no. 2 (1976): 141–52.

Famiglietti, Joseph, Mark Fraser, and Karin Newland (North Seattle Community College). "Delinquency Prevention: Four Developmentally Oriented Strategies." *Social Work in Education* 6, no. 4 (Summer 1984): 259–73.

Farnsworth, D. C. "Drug Use and Young People: Their Reasons, Our Reactions." In *Resource Book for Drug Abuse Education.* 2d ed. Washington, D.C.: National Clearing House of Drug Abuse Information, 1972.

Fearlemann, Mimi (Menninger Foundation). "Alcoholism: A Problem To Be Reckoned With." *Menninger Perspective* 6, no. 1 (Spring 1975): 4–9.

Federal Bureau of Investigation. *Crime in the United States, 1980: Uniform Crime Report.* Washington, D.C.: U.S. Government Printing Office, 1981.

Freud, Sigmund. *Civilization and Its Discontents.* Garden City, N.Y.: Doubleday, 1958.

Goode, E., ed. *Marijuana.* New York: Walter, 1969.

Hargens, Jurgan. "Family Orientation in West German Probation Agencies: Request or Reality?" *Partnerberatung* 20, nos. 2–3 (1983): 118–27.

Hartford, T. C. "Patterns of Alcohol Use Among Adolescents." *Psychiatric Opinion* 12 (1975): 17–21.

Hindman, Margaret (Hood College). "Child Abuse and Neglect: The Alcohol Connection." *Alcohol Health and Research World* 1, no. 3 (Spring 1977): 2–7.

Hunt, Leon, and Carl Chambers. *The Heroin Epidemics.* New York: Spectrum, 1976.

Jakalen, A. W. "Drug Use and the Adolescent." In *Understanding Adolescence: Current Developments in Adolescent Psychology.* 2d ed., edited by J. F. Adams. Boston: Allyn and Bacon, 1973.

Jares, M. C. "Personality Correlates and Antecedents of Drinking Patterns in Adult Males." *Journal of Consulting and Clinical Psychology* 32 (1968): 2–12.

Jellinek, E. M. *Phases in the Drinking History of Alcoholics.* New Haven, Conn.: Hillhouse Press, 1946.

Katchadourian, H. A. *The Biology of Adolescence.* San Francisco: Freeman, 1977.

Katz, P. "Treatment of Juvenile Delinquency." *Corrective Psychiatry and Journal of Social Therapy* 18, no. 2 (1972): 28–38.

Keller, Mark, and Carol Gurioli. *Statistics on Consumption of Alcohol and on Alcohol.* New Brunswick, N.J.: Rutgers Center of Alcohol Studies, 1973.

Kendel, D. B. "Inter and International Influences on Adolescent Marijuana Use." *Journal of Social Issues* 30 (1974): 107–35.

————. "Sequence and Stages in Patterns of Adolescent Drug Use." *Archives of General Psychiatry* 32 (1975): 923–32.

Lawn, John C. (Administrator: Drug Enforcement Administration). "Drugs in America—Our Problem, Our Solution." *Vital Speeches of the Day* 52, no. 11 (March 15, 1986).

Lawrence, T. S., and J. Velleman. "Correlates of Student Drug Use in a Suburban High School." *Psychiatry* 37 (1974): 129–36.

Leon, J. "Trends in Drug Use Among Young People in Oshawa: Prevalence and Responses." *Canada's Mental Health* 25 (1977): 6–10.

Levine, Edward, and Conrad Kozak (Loyola University). "Drug and Alcohol Use, Delinquency and Vandalism Among Upper Middle

Class Pre and Post Adolescents." *Journal of Youth and Adolescence* 8, no. 1 (March 1979): 91–105.

Levine, S. V. (Sunnybrook Medical Center, Toronto, California). "Alienation As an Effect of Adolescence." In *The Adolescent and Mood Disturbance.* Edited by Harvey Golombek and Barry D. Garfinkel. New York: International Universities Press, 1983.

Linder, Ronald, and Steven Lerner (California State University, San Francisco). "Self Medication: An Only Child Syndrome." *Journal of Psychedelic Drugs* 5, no. 1 (Fall 1972): 62–66.

Loker, J. O. *Student Alienation and Dissent.* Scarborough, Ontario: Prentice Hall, 1973.

Mead, Margaret. *Culture and Commitment.* New York: Doubleday, 1970.

Merton, Robert. *Social Theory and Social Structure.* 2d ed. New York: Free Press, 1968.

Mott, Joy, and N. H. Rathold. "Heroin Misuse and Delinquency in a New Town." *British Journal of Psychiatry* 128 (May 1976): 428–35.

Murphy, Brian, and Martha Shinyei (Canadian Penitentiary Service). "Cons and Straights: Comparative Free Behavior Rates of Twenty-Five Delinquents and Twenty-Five Non-Delinquents Matched for Age and Legal Occupation in British Columbia, Canada." *Canadian Journal of Criminology and Corrections* 18, no. 4 (Oct. 1976): 343–61.

Nathan, Peter E. (Rutgers University). "Failures in Prevention: Why We Can't Prevent the Devastating Effect of Alcoholism and Drug Abuse." *American Psychologist* 38, no. 4 (April 1983): 459–67.

National Clearing House for Drug Abuse Information. *Amphetamines.* Rockville, Md.: Alcohol, Drug Abuse, and Mental Health Administration Report, Series 28, no. 1 (Feb. 1974).

National Institute on Drug Abuse. *Sedative-Hypnotic Drugs: Risks and Benefits.* Washington, D.C.: U.S. Government Printing Office, 1972.

Noble, Ernest, ed. *Alcohol and Health: Third Special Report to the United States Congress.* Rockville, Md.: U.S. Public Health Service (June 1978).

Offer, Daniel, Richard Marohn, and Eric Ostrov (Michael Reese Hospital Institute for Psychiatric Research, Chicago, Ill.). "Delinquent and Normal Adolescents." *Comprehensive Psychiatry* 13, no. 4 (June 1972): 347–55.

Podolsky, Doug (Research Triangle Institute). "Economic Costs of Alcohol Abuse and Alcoholism." *Alcohol Health and Research World* 9, no. 2 (Winter 1984–85): 34–36.

Satterfield, James, Dennis Cantwell (Gateways Hospital, Los Angeles, California). "Psychopharmacology in the Prevention of Antisocial and Delinquent Behavior." *International Journal of Mental Health* 4, nos. 1–2 (Spring/Summer 1975): 227–37.

Schukit, M. A., and J. W. Russell (University of California at San Diego Medical School, Department of Psychiatry). "An Evaluation of Primary Alcoholics with Histories of Violence." *Journal of Clinical Psychiatry* 45, no. 1 (Jan. 1984): 3–6.

Schukit, Marc (University of Washington Alcoholism and Drug Abuse Institution). "Propoxyphene and Phencyclidine (PCP) Use in Adolescents." *Journal of Clinical Psychiatry* 39, no. 1 (Jan. 1978): 7–13.

Second Report of the National Commission on Marijuana and Drug Abuse. "Drug Use in America: Problems in Perspective." Washington, D.C.: U.S. Government Printing Office, 1973.

Serrone, D. M. "Over the Counter Drugs: A Challenge for Drug Education." *Journal of Drug Education* 3 (1973): 101–10.

Shade, Ruth, and Willard Hendrickson (University of Michigan Neuropsychiatric Institute). "Pill Culture Parents and Their Drug Using Teenagers: A New and Frightening Therapeutic Challenge." *American Journal of Orthopsychiatry* 41, no. 2 (1971): 297–98.

Steiningere, Edward H., Leon Lappel (Community Child Guidance Clinic, West Collingwood, New Jersey). "Group Therapy for Reluctant Juvenile Probationers and Their Parents." *Adolescence* 5, no. 17 (1970): 67–77.

Stephenson, Normal, Patrick Boudewyns, and Rudolph Lessing (V.A. Hospital, Nashville, Tennessee). *Journal of Drug Issues* 7, no. 2 (Spring 1977): 135–49).

Stivers, Richard. *A Hair of the Dog: Irish Drinking and the American Stereotype.* University Park, Penn.: Pennsylvania University Press, 1976.

Stumphauzer, Jerome, and Phillip Perez (University of Southern California Medical Center). "Learning To Drink: Peer Survey of Normal Adolescents." *International Journal of Addictions* 17, no. 8 (1982): 1363–72.

Tennent, Forrest (University of California in Los Angeles). "Child-hood Antecedents of Alcohol and Drug Abuse." *Dissertation Abstracts International.* Ann Arbor, Michigan.

Thompson, R. F. *Introduction to Physiological Psychology.* 2d ed. New York: Harper & Row, 1975.

U.S. Bureau of the Census. *Statistical Abstracts of the United States 1979. Washington, D.C.: U.S. Government Printing Office, 1980.*

Victor, H. R., J. C. Grossman, and R. Eisenman. "Openness to Experience and Marijuana Use in High School Students." *Journal of Consulting and Clinical Psychology* 41 (1973): 78–85.

Weidman, Arthur (Family Services Association Professional Services, Indianapolis, Indiana). "The Compulsive Adolescent Substance Abuser: Psychological Differentiation and Family Process." *Journal of Drug Education* 13, no. 2 (1983): 161–72.

Yancey, W. S. "Drug Use and Attitudes of High School Students." *Pediatrics* 50 (1972): 739–45.